DIVINATION
ORACLES & OMENS

DIVINATION
ORACLES & OMENS

Edited by Michelle Aroney and David Zeitlyn

BODLEIAN
LIBRARY
PUBLISHING

Falcolanarius · Acar · Monedula cato? · Corbellus

Doctel · Alcolanariuf · Katar

P·Ú·F·u· Cõde re amilla an poïít re cupari·l'ñ· uel ñ· Itead regem frãc · Gelzem? clari en amu

P·Ú·F·iu· Cõde egro si poïít euadere ut ñ·Ite ad regé belze nt·

P·Ú·F·u· Rõde euadam re li poít te uit non·Ite ad regem clarite ru̅ amã·

P·Ú·F·uiii· an cet bonu̅ ue gr dõu̅ uel·ñ· Ite ad regé cur co

P·Ú·F·ir· Cõ an cet bonu̅ ue gr dõu̅ ut ñ· Ite ad rege Pe

regem Batllo nic̅·

CONTENTS

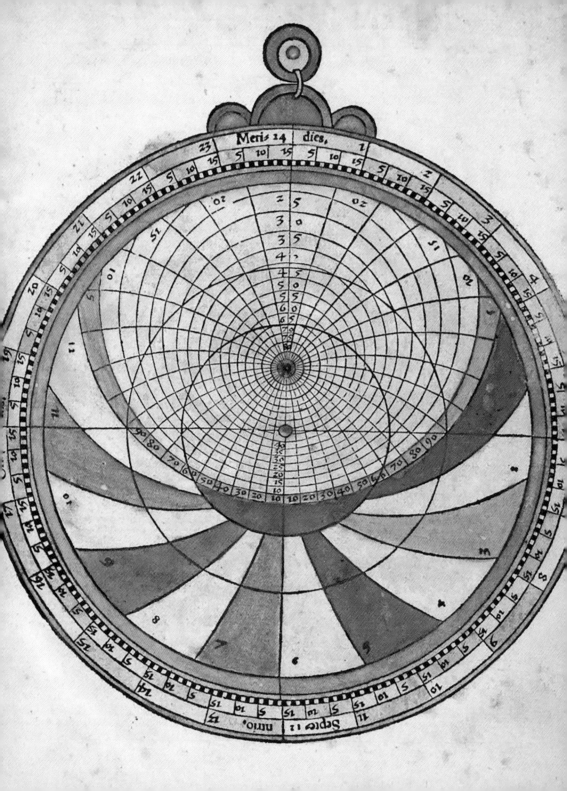

INTRODUCTION

DIVINATION IN THE WORLD: MAKING SENSE, USING AUGURY

Michelle Aroney and David Zeitlyn

The past, present and future are full of mysteries: inscrutable secrets about our lives and the lives of those around us that are difficult to uncover through unassisted human understanding. Every day we confront the limits of our own capabilities when it comes to the enigmas of the past and present and the uncertainties of the future. Making decisions in the face of the unknowable is a daily dilemma. Across history and around the world, humans have addressed this by using techniques that promise to unveil the concealed, disclosing knowledge that offers answers to private or shared dilemmas. Techniques of divination come in a wide variety of different forms, but they all offer insights into underlying truths that lie outside of our normal grasp. Discovering, or uncovering, this hidden information can help diagnose present problems and empower us to make decisions about future actions.

People make difficult decisions all the time. Most of us just get on with it and decide, whether or not we can give reasons for why and how we have come to opt one way or another. Years later some may regret their decisions, but many important decisions seem to pass the test of hindsight. Other people seek special help in making their decisions or in justifying or explaining them. These are

Detail of paper astrolabe from Johann Stöffler's *Elucidatio fabricae vsusque astrolabii* (see Fig. 9, pp. 32–3).

9

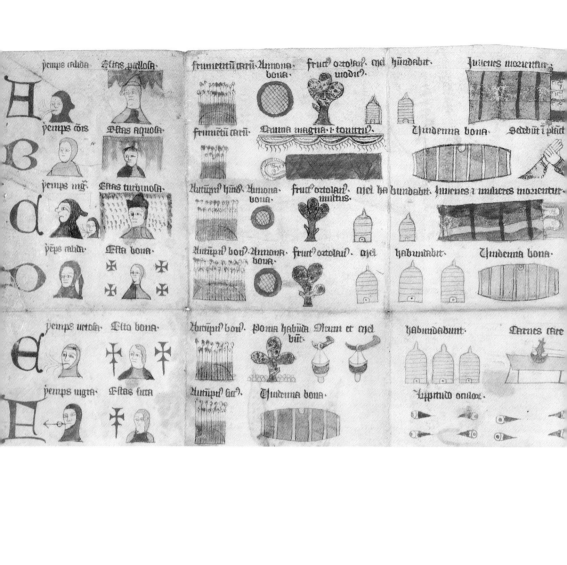

yemps calida · Elras piallofa · frumentū carū Amona bona · fruct ozolual · mel inodic · hūndabit · Iuuenes mozientur ·

yemps cōis · Eltas aquofa · frumētu carū · vauna magna · t tonitru · Uindemia bona · Scribūt ī plact ·

yemps migr · Eras turbinofa · Autūpñ hūd · Amona bona · fruct ozolanū multus · mel habundabit · Iuuenes t mulieres morientur ·

yēps calida · Elta bona · Autūpñ bon · Amona bona · fruct ozolan · mel · habūdabit · Uindemia bona ·

yemps urtola · Elta bona · Autūpñ bon · Poma habūda būt · fleum et mel · habundabunt · Carnes care ·

yemps migra · Estas ficca · Autūpñ fic · Uindemia bona · Tẏpmud oculoz ·

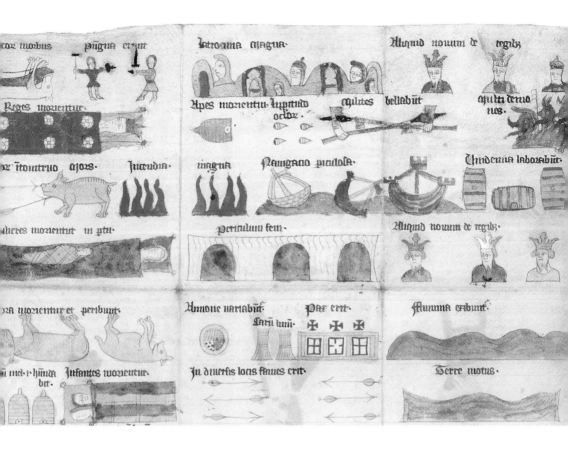

cor morbus   pugna erunt   latronia magna·   Aliquid nouum de regibz

Reges morientur·   Apes morientur· tempestud oribz·   milites bellabūt   multi terno tur.

ce tonitruo mors·   Incendia·   magna   Nauigaco pitolosa·   Innerna laborabūt

heres morientur in pti·   Periculum fem·   Aliquid nouum de regibz·

ra morientur et peribunt·   Annone variabit   Pax erit·   flumina exibunt·

Larū hui·

i mel · i · hunia bit· Infantes morientur·   In diuersis locis fames erit·   Terre motus·

1 A late fourteenth-century English collection of forecasts, designed to be folded up as a portable booklet. Seven rows of prognostications for seven years run horizontally across the page, offering predictions about, for instance, the weather in winter and summer (illustrated by men's heads) and whether each year could expect good harvests (sieves), abundant fruit (trees), much honey (beehives) and thunderstorms (a corpse beneath fiery clouds).

and have been the clients of diviners, the querents seeking answers.

In this book, we present short introductions to some examples of divination from around the world and at different periods of history. We seek to illustrate the variety of different ways that have been devised in most human cultures to find answers to hard, arcane questions. What we offer here is thus a sampler, rather than a comprehensive catalogue, of techniques used in a variety of historical and contemporary cultures to access occult knowledge – where occult (from the Latin *occultus*) simply means 'hidden', 'secret' or 'covered up'.

What Is Divination?

We use the term 'divination' to mean the methods used to find answers to arcane questions, often (though not always) about the future. Some of the hardest questions are actually about the past or about explanations from the past for present troubles. Clients of divination often seek an answer to the question of what caused the problem they are currently facing: 'Why am I [or my family member] ill?', 'What caused this accident?' or 'Who stole from me?' In other words, what is the hidden cause or meaning of this event? Seeking insights into the future is a central part of divinatory practice, but so are questions about the past and the present. Crucially, divination provides not only answers to these questions but also guidance in light of them: 'Knowing this, what should I do now?' At least as far back as ancient Mesopotamia, some 5,000 years ago, the same kinds of questions were asked of specialist practitioners who employed techniques that could provide compelling answers.

Though it is often deadly serious, divination can sometimes be approached more light-heartedly. In the

West (and elsewhere), many dismiss divination as a sort of superstition, even if some of those same people might occasionally consult their horoscopes more or less seriously. Forms of divining are widespread in Western culture, from children's games predicting future marriage partners to attempts to predict the winner of the FIFA World Cup from the movements of an octopus. Toy shops sell divination gadgets – Magic 8 balls, fortune fish and ouija boards – and divination is a common theme in popular culture. Not only does J.K. Rowling's Hogwarts School teach courses in unfogging the future but forms of supernatural skill are quite often crucial to the plots of stories and films. For example, the original Oedipus myth starts with an attempt to evade the prediction of an oracle, Arthur Savile's crime in the Oscar Wilde short story is a response to a palm reading, and various forms of prediction feature in many stories including the James Bond film *Live and Let Die* (1973) and Philip Pullman's *His Dark Materials* series (1995–2000). In many places different types of divination are regarded in diverse ways, one being dismissed as just a game or a toy, while another might be taken very seriously indeed. A client may start asking a question jokingly or flippantly but then find that they cannot treat the answer they have been given as just a joke. One can find juxtapositions of attitudes in the same cultural tradition, and the same incongruities can even be present in individuals. A cynic may trip over an uncannily knowing reading, or a devotee of divination may find that months have gone by without a consultation. Patterns of usage reflect and echo patterns of life. Often there are gradations, shades of seriousness, a continuum of differences that moves from play to serious consideration of life-changing decisions.

2 'The Original Fortune Teller, or, Chinese Wheel of Fortune', by A. Park, an engraver and publisher in the nineteenth century. The wheel may have been used in Victorian parlour games.

THE ORIGINAL

UNE TELLER

THE WHEEL OF FORTUNE.

ARK. 47. Leonard Street, Finsbury, London.

Divination also sits on another spectrum, at one end of which sit scientific forms of prediction. It has been commonplace since the 2008 Global Financial Crisis to claim that economics seems to function much like astrology in that, when it comes to prediction, the success rates of both can leave a lot to be desired. Other forms of scientific forecasting – such as epidemiology – are of course far more reliable, although when the weather turns out to be worse (or better) than anticipated we might quibble about meteorology. What all these practices of forecasting and prediction have in common is that they are stochastic arts, a technical term derived from the Greek *stókhos* meaning 'aim' or 'guess'. Historically, the term has referred to the practice of conjecture, especially in relation to matters that are in their nature variable and uncertain. The ancient notion of a stochastic art included medicine and navigation as well as astrology; it referred to bodies of knowledge and practice that involved skilled guesswork and the notion of aiming rather than hitting. Because they dealt with variable materials, a measure of failure was to be expected. But, while even the best physician today cannot guarantee a successful outcome for their patient, most of us nevertheless conclude that medicine is still very useful. In one sense, it is the cultural map of knowledge in any historical context that differentiates and separates divination from scientific forms of prediction.

As the contributions to this book show, techniques of divination come in many forms. Divination often involves the interpretation of patterns or clues – in natural things such as seeds, bones, guts, birds and celestial bodies, as well as in human-made or manipulated things such as cards, dice, images and candles – by means of skilled and usually standardized methods. Divination

3 A brass astrolabe made by Muhammad Muqim in Lahore, Pakistan, in 1643/4 CE (1053 AH). Astrolabes had a great variety of uses, including determining planetary positions, which was essential for casting horoscopes.

may also involve more direct commerce with non-human others such as deities, demons or ancestors. Some of the forms of divination presented in this book call for the use of ceremonial paraphernalia, sacred objects such as altars, candles and texts, or even mathematical tools such as astrolabes and astronomical tables. Diviners themselves are of all ages and genders, and often hold a similar societal role to a priest or a physician; in some cultures they can be one and the same person. Sometimes individuals can divine for themselves, adopting the roles of both diviner and client, but in some traditions auto-divination is frowned upon if not explicitly forbidden.

Divination can be practised in many different places. Some practitioners work from home, some in a clinic and some only at particular sacred or special sites. Others may be itinerant diviners, who travel around and set up shop for a while in a place before moving on. While it was once considered radically modern to consult a diviner remotely, successive technological developments in some cultures have helped to normalize this. For example, although it is still a rare occurrence, Mambila diviners in Cameroon sometimes conduct consultations for friends and relatives in far-flung cities using mobile phones, and are also now accessible online. Today, Google Play and the Apple App Store have many, many apps for divination. Some of these enable users to generate astrological charts themselves or offer guidance for reading the *Yijing*. Many apps are self-contained, while others are gateways that facilitate bespoke consultations with human diviners through WhatsApp messages, Zoom sessions or other platforms. Some professionals disapprove of such developments while others encourage them.

In this introductory chapter, we outline some of the ways in which scholars in a variety of fields have tried to understand the history and to analyse the practice of divination. The scholarly study of divination is a fraught field. There are definitional challenges, and difficult and confrontational questions abound. In compiling this book and curating the Bodleian Library exhibition it accompanies, we have tried to be as inclusive as possible about what we recognize as a form of divination. For example, we have included astrology, which some will disagree with. As this is a collaboration between an anthropologist and a historian, we approach divination from a critical, scholarly perspective. We have avoided entirely the divisive normative questions about whether the practices presented here are 'true', whether they work or if people need to believe in them for them to work.

Historically, the critical (as in analytical) study of divination has often gone hand in hand with criticism (or downright condemnation) of divination. Perhaps the most famous critique of divination – Cicero's *On Divination*, from the first century CE – is also arguably one of the first scholarly studies of divination. Presented as a dialogue between Cicero and his brother Quintus, the book debates the merits and possibilities of different forms of divination used in Rome and nearby nations. In the process Cicero compares and analyses astrology, augury (divination from the behaviour of birds), haruspicy (from entrails), oneiromancy (from dreams), oracles (possession by the gods) and sortilege (from the casting of lots).

In the dialogue, Cicero is deeply sceptical of all forms of divination, while Quintus is positive about their effectiveness and usefulness. Quintus explains that in the world there are signs of future events, and that because of their skill or their relationship to the gods, some people

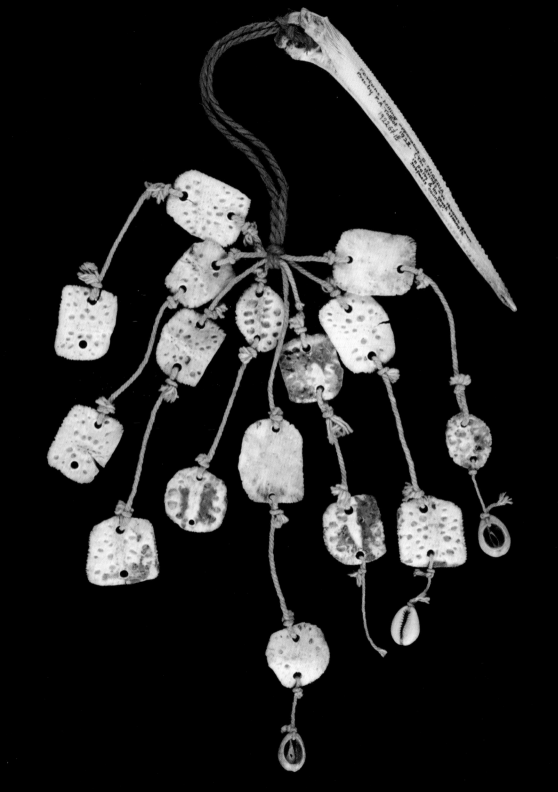

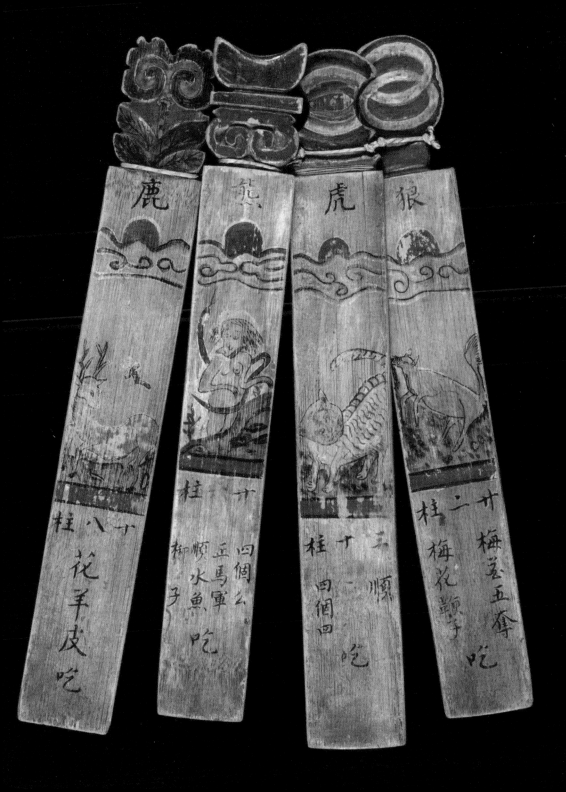

are able to 'recognize those signs and foretell events before they occur'. Ignoring or 'failing to seek out' these signs, Quintus argues, means that we are liable to 'run into awful disasters'. Making the most of these patterns, meanwhile, allows human beings to 'approach very near to the power of gods'.[1] While we may avoid siding with either Cicero or Quintus, their discussion raises a number of points that guide the discussion in the rest of this chapter. As we have already noted, for all its enduring popularity and usage, divination has always attracted some more than others: many people make important and difficult decisions without its assistance, but many others do ask for help. It is these people, and their diviners, that are the subject of this book.

Diagnosis and Prediction

We use normal and trivial types of prediction every day. For example, we routinely estimate that it will shortly be safe to cross the road when the next car has passed, or that this person is about to stop talking so we can take our conversational turn. The success of such commonplace predictions bolsters the sense of certainty clients find in divinatory pronouncements. There is nothing unusual about prediction, for all the problems it poses for philosophers. Philosophical assessments of the results of divination tend to depend on the tense of the pronouncements, and thus distinguish between two uses or aspects of divination: diagnosis that looks back and forward-looking prognosis or prediction. Actual divinatory practice often covers both, but the distinction is helpful because the two aspects have very different philosophical implications.

Diagnosis primarily concerns the past. It takes an existing state of affairs and attempts to unpick its (often

previous pages

left **4** Divination apparatus from southern Nigeria, made before 1922. The strings are thrown in pairs, and the rough and smooth surfaces counted: odd or even numbers allow a verse to be selected, in a system similar to *Ifá* (for which see pp. 161–4).

right **5** Painted bamboo divining tablets, made before 1922. One is selected from a bundle and its text is interpreted to answer the question.

deeply obscure) causal foundations. Diagnosis seeks to establish *which* of a variety of possible causes has been the active agent in a particular case. It is tied to the case at hand and looks backwards into the past. The language used to describe such divinatory usage often refers to clarification, uncovering the hidden or shining light onto dark obscurity, often to the astonishment of the layperson who is not privy to the techniques. These are the techniques of diagnosis, not of prediction.

In contrast, and as philosophers since Aristotle have worried, prediction raises conundrums that do not affect diagnosis. Prediction seeks to identify future scenarios – possible outcomes. In divination and other forms of predictive technology, there is often a kind of double subjunctive at play. First, a prediction is uncertain at the moment of utterance, since the future is never actual at *that* moment; the utterance is hypothetical. Then there is often an implicit second stage of hypothecating, for implicit in many divinatory outcomes is the qualifying clause that if nothing is done *this* will happen. Yet this (usually bad) outcome may be avoided by performing a specified action.

While the distinction between diagnosis and prognosis is profound in philosophical terms, in practice the two shade into one another. Thus, a diagnostic judgement will have predictive implications. For example, there is an element of diagnosis when deciding what medical treatment to seek (for *this* ailment the best thing to do is *that*), but there is also a predictive aspect (doing *this* will successfully resolve *that* problem). In other words, to plan for the future we have to understand the past. In a few celebrated instances it is clear that the one implies the other: in some cases a diagnosis has clear, unambiguous prognostic implications. An example is

Huntington's disease, where the diagnosis of a particular genetic defect allows for a confident prediction of the later onset of the disease. However, these are exceptions, and the implications of a medical diagnosis (especially when it is couched in the probabilistic language of risk) are mostly uncertain when it is applied to an individual patient. More commonly, a diagnosis can lead to different outcomes depending on what people do next: their actions in response to the diagnosis have consequences. This can make it hard to assess the accuracy of the predictions that may follow. A further complication in medicine is that, while most people recover from most illnesses, some have illnesses that are difficult not only to diagnose but also to treat, and these patients often seek second or third opinions, sometimes moving backwards and forwards between doctors and diviners.

The distinction between prediction and diagnosis may not be obvious to practitioners, and certainly has not been important for previous academic researchers. Part of the reason the distinction seems to collapse is that success in diagnosis is measured by its apparent predictive efficacy. By correctly identifying the problem we can plan how to solve it. If the problem is solved, we subsequently *infer* that the diagnosis was correct. For most clients, once the problem has been solved the details of what those problems were, let alone their aetiology, become irrelevant and not worthy of further enquiry. Yet the action taken may have remedied a problem that had a different set of causes, or the problem may have rectified itself independently of any actions taken (as happens in many self-limiting medical conditions). As much medical research testifies, the success of a treatment does not necessarily justify the explanation given for how the treatment works.

Technical and Inspired

In their debate, Quintus and Cicero distinguish between two types of divination: one based on nature, the other based on art. What they meant was that some types of divination involve a form of possession, whereby a god or spirit possesses, inspires or talks through the diviner. Others, meanwhile, involve art, in the sense of skill, craft or technique. In these types of divination, a wholly human operator uses established procedures to access the required information. This could involve tossing a basket of objects in the air so that the spirits can determine the objects that land on top, shuffling a pack of cards, opening a sacred text at random or looking at the pattern of coffee grounds left after someone has finished their drink.

We might call the first type *inspired* and the second *technical*. Our coverage in this book tilts towards technical divination, where knowledge is communicated using signs, omens and technical procedures, perhaps involving the casting of objects or shuffling of cards rather than through the possession of a human medium. These procedures might allow for communion with the ancestors, as in Mesoamerica, or with demons, as in medieval Europe. We do, however, include some instances of more directly inspired divination, such as the examples provided by ancient Greek oracles, medieval necromancy and Lunda basket divination.

This distinction between inspired and technical divination, already well established by the time Cicero used it in the first century BCE, at first sight seems helpful. On the face of it, someone is either possessed or not (though possession may be faked), but a procedure may be done incorrectly, or a technical diviner may make mistakes, which can be used to explain why their results are said to be wrong. However, in many cases there are procedures to be followed for someone to become possessed, so there are often technical aspects to possession rituals. Many of the musical instruments, rattles and drums associated with divination fall into this category.

Thus, while Cicero's distinction seems clear, it can be less than helpful. If the issue is the source of the knowledge or the originator of the message delivered by the diviner, there may be no difference at all between the two types of divination. Whether the spirit possesses someone or speaks through cards, they are the ultimate source of the message and should be trusted, unlike possibly deceitful or manipulative humans. Lunda diviners in Zambia, among many others using similar or very different methods, say that they are in contact with spirits when they shake the baskets of objects whose patterns they then interpret. Is this inspired or technical divination? Surely it is both.

Explanation and Experiment

We can also make a distinction between systems where there is a local account of why the divination technique works and systems where there is no such explanation but the fact that it works is taken as answer enough. Premodern European and Ottoman astrology, for example, had sophisticated philosophical and mathematical theories for why the stars held clues about the past, present and future, theories based on the writings of ancient thinkers such as Ptolemy. But sometimes there are only relatively simple explanations for why some divinatory methods are used – such as that the gods speak through this person – and at other times there is no explanation at all and we are simply told

6 A zodiac man from a medieval English manuscript, c.1440. These standardized figures illustrated which zodiac signs were associated with particular parts of the body, for example Pisces with the feet and Aries with the head. Theories about the association of the heavens with the body were important in premodern European medicine.

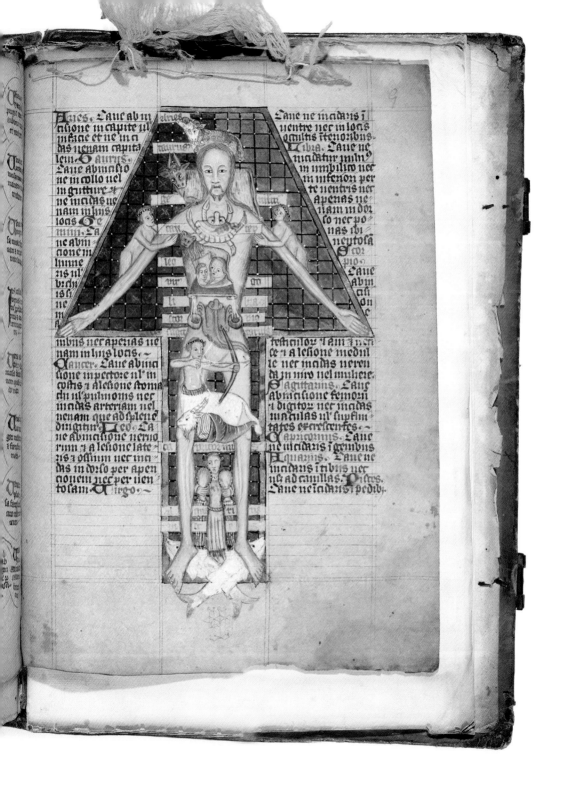

Aries. Caue ab in-
cisione in capite ul-
neficie et ne inci-
das uenam capita-
lem. Taurus.
Caue ab incisio-
ne in collo uel
in gutture et
ne incidas ue-
nam in huis
locis. Gemi-
ni. Ca-
ue ab incisi-
one in
humo-
ris ul'
brach-
iis
ne
incid
as
ne
na

Caue ne incidas i
uentre nec in locis
ocultis iterioribus.
Libra. Caue ne
incidatur in lumb'
in umbilico nec
in iferion per-
te uentris nec
Apenas ue-
niam in dor-
so nec po-
nas ibi
uentosa
Scor-
pio
Caue
ab in-
cisi-
on
ne

mbus nec aperias ue-
nam in huis locis.
Cancer. Caue ab inci-
sione in pectore ul' in
costis et alesione stoma-
chi ul' pulmonis nec
incidas arteriam uel
uenam que ad splene
dirigitur. Leo. Ca-
ue ab incisione neruo-
rum et alesione late-
ris et ossium nec inci-
das in dorso per apen-
cionem nec per uen-
tosam. Virgo.

testiculos. Tam i incr-
ce et alesione medul-
le uel incidas uerec-
da in uiro uel muliere.
Sagittarius. Caue
ab incisione femori
et digitor' nec incidas
macul's ul' superflui-
tates excrescentes.
Capricornus. Caue
ne uicidas i genibus
Aquarius. Caue ne
incidas i tibiis uel
nec ad camillas. Pisces.
Caue ne incidas i pedib'.

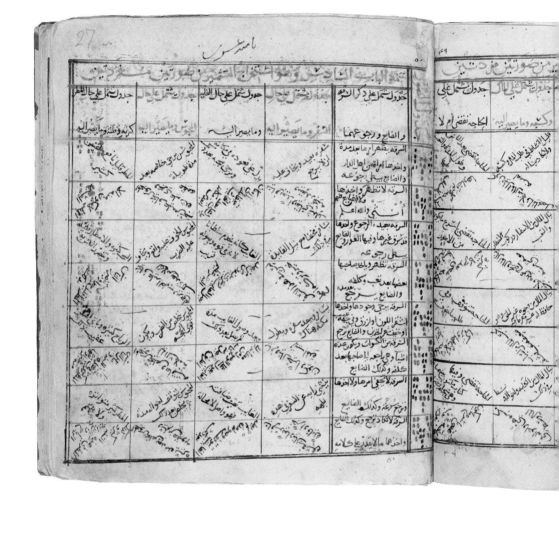

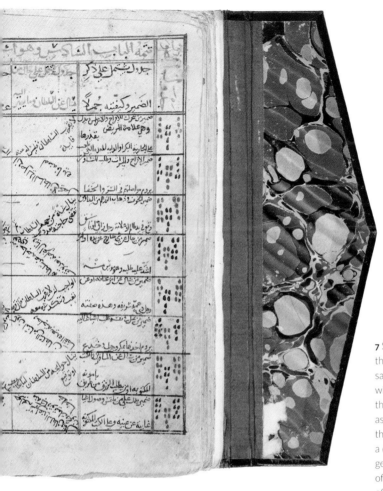

7 Sand-cutting geomancy involves the use of a board covered with sand, which is marked at random with a stylus. The practitioner then uses geomantic tables, such as that pictured here, to interpret the marks in the sand to answer a question. The tables show the geomantic figures in the form of dots together with a number of questions, including the outcome of court cases, whether monetary gains will be made, whether trade will be successful and what the weather will be (*Ibn al-Maḥfūf, Kitāb al-Muthallathāt fī ʿilm al-raml* (*The Book of the Triads: On Geomancy*)).

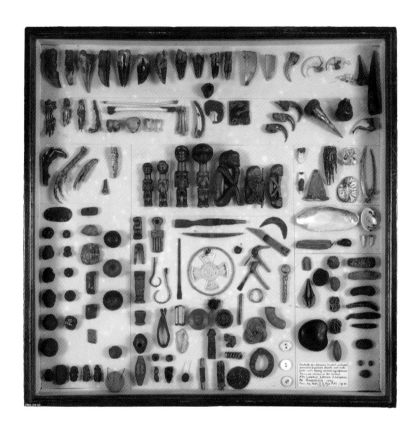

8 Contents of a Zambian diviner's basket, including wooden figures, shells, seeds, nuts, buttons, glass and parts of animals (made before 1930). The diviner shakes the basket, and their reading is based on the objects that have risen to the top.

that it works. Here past successes justify continuing use. Systematic record-keeping is very rare, and few diviners follow up on their consultations to find out what their clients did with the results of their divination. Some clients return to tell diviners that the results of their consultations were positive, and this bolsters their sense of their own accuracy.

Confusion is often caused by researchers who persist in asking questions about origins and sources until their informants provide answers, even though the explanations may not be widely shared. There are grey areas too. Among Mambila diviners, there is a myth that explains why the procedures of spider divination are necessary: in the distant past the spiders used to speak but they lost the power of speech because a spider showed a human the path to the village of the dead. What such myths do not explain is how the spider got its uncanny knowledge in the first place. When asked, Mambila diviners refer to ancestors but do not offer an explanation; there is no account of how spiders and ancestors relate to each other. Some things are explained, while others are not. Indeed, practitioners' explanations of a form of divination may not be what their clients find puzzling or intriguing about it, and researchers, historians and anthropologists may have very different questions, perhaps provoked by comparison with other systems – questions that cannot always be answered.

Cicero and Quintus confronted a similar problem. Ancient advocates of divination, Cicero pointed out, were 'influenced more by actual results than convinced by reason'.[2] In his defence of divination, Quintus explained what this meant: the theories underpinning methods of divination, which explained why a certain technique worked, did not matter so much as that it actually worked for the people involved. As he told his brother, 'You ask why everything happens. You have a perfect right to ask, but that is not the point at issue now. The question is: does it happen or does it not?'[3] Scholars have often made a similar point. From the perspective of the clients of divination, the explanation and epistemic status of divined knowledge is less important than its practical efficacy. In this context, what matters is not so much *why* the given answer might be right but whether the answer is helpful or meaningful. As the quotation from *Hamlet* put it, 'the readiness is all'.

following pages

9 This paper astrolabe appeared in a 1535 edition of an important Renaissance book, Johann Stöffler's *Elucidatio fabricae vsusque astrolabii*. The paper instrument was probably intended to be cut out and assembled for use.

Expertise and Empiricism

Even if some forms of divination are not given a complex or nuanced philosophical explanation, their practice is nevertheless premised on the skill and expertise of the practitioner on the one hand, and the success of their methods on the other. Indeed, divination techniques are empirical in that their practitioners have long collected data that sheds light on their efficacy. As already noted, this may not be as systematic as we might like, and perhaps only reports of success are recorded. Be that as it may, these reports and their records can serve as justifications for diviners of many different systems, demonstrating to their satisfaction that their clients have been helped. As Quintus argued, divination had grown into an art 'through the repeated observation and recording of almost countless instances in which the same results have been preceded by the same signs'.[4]

Such record-keeping often contributes to the continued reform and improvement of the art. In medieval and Renaissance Europe, for example, astrologers kept records of natural and human events, comparing their occurrence to the movements of the heavenly bodies in an effort to refine existing astrological theories. As a result of such practices of refinement, some divinatory texts changed over time, and not only in the European tradition: developments leading to changes to the manual have, for example, also been found in the Tibetan tradition. In Cameroon, spider divination is tested on a regular basis with questions that have an obviously right or wrong answer (e.g., 'Am I here alone?'). Spiders that fail the test are no longer used for divination. As Sophie Page points out in her chapter on necromancy, in the medieval period necromantic rituals were called

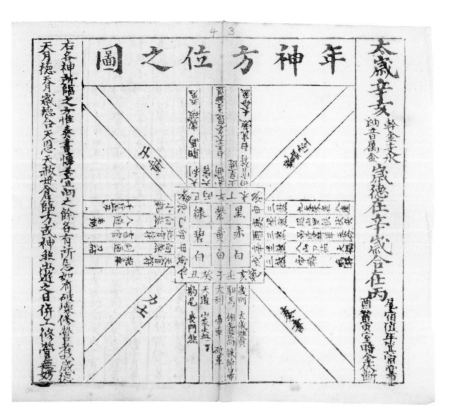

年神方位之圖

experimenta, for they were seen as techniques that could be improved with repeated use. In this sense each instance of divination was an experiment in service of the greater aim of better results.

In many forms of divination, the skill of the diviner matters a great deal. If an astrologer makes a prediction that turns out to be false, for example, they can blame their own failings rather than any underlying problems with astrology; in other words, the fault lies with the artist rather than the art. After all, divination requires a specialist skill set and, typically, training of some

10 A hexagram used in Chinese *Yijing*, 1671. A hexagram, representing a particular cosmic condition, is selected by picking up yarrow stalks (or tossing coins) and then counting whether the client has picked an odd or even number, thus generating a line of the hexagram. This is repeated until the full hexagram is produced.

kind, often an apprenticeship. Practitioners of Yorùbá *Ifá* divination, for example, spend years learning a structured corpus of poetry, a repository of verse that is then interpreted to provide an answer to a client's problem. The *Yijing* also has a large corpus that used to be learnt before anyone could practise as a diviner, although this has changed with the printing of the *Yijing* verses.

In other systems, illness or other forms of affliction are signs of having been chosen by gods or deities as a legitimate diviner. This process can be managed by initiation into the group of diviners, a chosen few, not all of whom necessarily practise as diviners. In short, some people choose to train as diviners, while others are chosen. In some systems there are more or less elaborate initiations and apprenticeships, and are thus more or less institutionalized, while in others individual desire and natural ability are sufficient. Practitioners need to be skilled not just in the detailed practice of the system in question (such as learning the *Ifá* verses or, in ancient Mesopotamia, learning how to sacrifice the goat whose liver will be examined as an omen) but also in interpreting the results. Letting a client choose a verse from the Bible or Qur'an (a technique often called *Sortes* or *bibliomancy*) does not seem to demand external knowledge or expertise, but the selected verse must then be interpreted to provide answers, and that is not an easy task.

11 The *Dīvān-i Ḥāfiẓ* (*Divan of Hafiz*) is an illuminated collection of poetic texts written by the medieval Iranian poet Hafez. It has long been used in Iran for bibliomancy, by extracting omens from the text on which the eye lands when the book is opened at random.

Patterns of popularization in many cultures have made way for more opportunities for auto-divination, as clients are able to learn the basics of these techniques themselves and use them in private to answer their own questions. With the arrival of the printing press in Europe, for instance, the basics of learned astrology, which were previously reserved for the initiated (in most

وفی پیرہ العجز

وتقدس پس نقدس پس محلی
فلیک معنا وصورت وخیالا

وتوحد عن السمات نعوتا
وتفرد عن الصفات حصالا

واطوی سبع الطباق طی محل
ورتفع عن جمیعهن کمالا

کبرا لمعدد و رایت بدولا
بهل لمعدد وسهت ت هلا لا

انقباض من اشارة

اولی بج نوحید الا با ایها الساقی
ارخی سلمة عنی عن قیدی یا طلا قی

بجام حرف توحیدم بدنسان کن ازنو
کار فانی شوم فانی بربا باقی شوم باقی

وشربی هیما یا کلاس پس من حیاه
وعطرنی بریا و زو وا یا هل ابو تی

تویی محی بصال من جمل من جمحی فی قلبی جمعین
اما نطری علی ما نظر ه دای با بی بی

تویی محی بصال من فقد و جد من لل زمن مشتاقی
اما نطری علی ما نظر ه دای یا اسمایی حا اخلا قی

cases those with university training), began to be shared in more accessible manuals, usually in the vernacular, so that more and more people could produce (comparably basic) astrological prognostications themselves. The *Yijing* was popularized in China more than a thousand years ago when the first books about it appeared and started to circulate. Likewise, the reading of tarot cards does not necessarily require an external practitioner, for individuals can use the cards themselves to prompt reflection about their own lives.

Some diviners simply offer advice in their consultations, leaving their clients or other experts to implement their guidance. But other diviners also offer to perform the rituals, sacrifices or treatments suggested by the divinatory response. In such cases there can be a perceived conflict of interest between the practice of divination and action taken on its advice. Such conflicts are clearly visible to both clients and diviners alike, and are sometimes openly and explicitly discussed. They are commonly referred to in explanations of why someone could have consulted divination but didn't, or why they did so but decided not to follow the counsel of divination. Some whole approaches to divination address this issue. Biblical *Sortes* involves a client choosing a verse from the Bible at random. As described above, basket diviners in many African systems put many objects in a basket, then toss them up in the air repeatedly and interpret the objects that finally come to the top. Practitioners of these and other systems make clear that the randomizing process prevents them from manipulating or interfering with the results, thereby allowing the deities to send a message (including by ultimately directing the choice of a scriptural passage or the arrangement of the objects in a basket) or the natural order of the universe to become discernible.

These sorts of explanations should not be taken as denying that randomness exists or that events may happen by chance, although such claims are sometimes also made. They can protect human operators from accusations of self-interested interference in the results. Often what is most important is for the diviner to visibly and demonstrably make it clear that they are not influencing the results. They may speak the results but the source of the utterance is *other*. The diviner is but a messenger. An example of this is the way many readers of cards start by saying 'The cards say…'. Implicit in such statements is the uninvolvedness of the diviner, a denial that they have any interest in the outcome.

Clients and Consultations

As researchers, we are as concerned with the individuals who make use of divination as we are with the diviners. In historical and contemporary cultures, people of all backgrounds and from all walks of life – from agricultural workers to princes and presidents – have consulted and continue to consult diviners. The clients who seek answers from diviners may consult them regularly, or only when they find themselves at a crossroads or in a crisis. Either way, clients are typically seeking not merely information but also guidance. In this book, we regard divination as a technology that assists decision-making, for the people who consult diviners are typically seeking answers that will help them to make decisions or to legitimize decisions that they have already made, thus putting their minds at ease. In this way, consultations function much like therapy. Today many people read their horoscope not only to better understand themselves but also to improve themselves and their lives. Divination consultations of various kinds involve conversations in which diviners and their clients work together to reach a mutually satisfactory outcome.

The clients of diviners may be individuals or corporations, groups and businesses; they may even be representatives of states. Consultations may occur in private or in public, whether in open with an audience or group of onlookers or more formally in the glare of the public sphere. These issues may make no difference to how the divination system is practised in the abstract, but they make a large difference to how a consultation works in practice. Even the simple distinction between private and public consultations makes a difference because, where there is an audience of onlookers, some of whom may be knowledgeable about the divination system being used, it is likely to affect how the diviner explains what they are doing and how they have arrived at the results. If the diviner knows that someone in the audience may be in a position to challenge the details of their practice, it may help create an orthodoxy of practice, that is, a widely shared understanding of how it should be done. An example may be the recitation of verses of *Ifá* where it is possible that another *babaláwo* may be present at a consultation, someone who may correct a misremembering of the verse selected. This is very different from the secret (certainly private) questioning regarding affairs of state from President Reagan's use (via his wife) of an astrologer (Joan Quigley) or ancient Greek states consulting the oracle at Delphi before embarking on a war.

Historically, diviners have often been closely connected to the administration of states. Cicero spoke of how the state hired diviners for the administration of public affairs, and long before this, in ancient Mesopotamia, a city could be a client of practitioners of extispicy (divination by the study of the entrails of a sacrificed animal). This was not unique to the ancient world. In the Ottoman Empire, astrologers had permanent official positions in court, their role being to make forecasts about war and peace, navigation and imperial expansion, famine and plague and, crucially, the life of the ruler. The same was true of many regimes in late medieval and Renaissance Europe. However, the perceived accuracy of divination was always double-edged. In the Bamoun state of western Cameroon, the ruler Sultan Njoya converted to Islam and invented his own writing system in the early twentieth century. Using this script he wrote the *History and Customs of the Bamoun* (*c.*1910), a text that lists new legislation and repealed laws, including the following:

16. If one consulted a diviner on the subject of an important man who was ill, and if one affirmed that he would not die, then were he to die the person who had consulted the diviner was also killed.

17. Those who consult the spider die.[5]

Moral: the *clients* of bad or mistaken diviners could be punished or even put to death! As it was understood locally, this law was not concerned with errors of divination, for Bamoun spiders do not lie. Instead, another law, which was repealed by Njoya, restricted the depiction of spiders as decorative motifs on bedposts, and spider divination was banned for being potentially treasonable.[6] That the health and safety of the ruler could be discovered through spider divination meant that, to preserve state secrets, its use had to be prohibited.

Similar examples can be found throughout much of human history. In seventeenth-century Italy, after a prominent astrologer predicted his death, Pope Urban

VIII issued a bull against the practice of astrology, especially predictions of the death of popes, princes or their families. The issue here is not so much with the epistemic status of the information produced via divination as about its subversive potential.

Perennial Questions

It is one thing to consider what methods have been used in divination and quite another to think about what these methods are used for. What are the questions that those consulting divination want to have answered, irrespective of the techniques used to provide answers? It may be that some questions are best asked of different types of divination. All that gets recorded about a system of divination is often the techniques or procedures used, while the questions these techniques are used to answer, which may be particular to the time and place of asking, may not be as well documented.

However, the historical record sometimes comes through on this front. The Bodleian Library, for example, has records of thousands of questions that were asked of the English astrologers Richard Napier and Simon Forman in the sixteenth and early seventeenth centuries. These questions range from queries about relationships ('Should I marry this person?', 'Am I the father of this child?' or 'Will my partner be faithful?') and personal affairs ('Is this rumour true?', 'Do I have secret enemies?' or 'What does this dream mean?') to business affairs ('Should I employ this person?', 'Should I sell this house?' or 'Should I take this job?') and more worldly events ('Will my country go to war?' or 'What will the weather be next week?'), the most common queries being medical. These questions, the answers to which are perennially sought after, have been and are still asked of diviners around the world.

12 The lavishly produced *Astronomicum Caesareum* (1540) contains numerous *volvelles*, paper instruments designed to enable the user to determine the positions of the planets in the heavens, primarily for the purpose of casting horoscopes. The sky volvelle pictured here is illustrated with constellations, including the signs of the Zodiac.

Remēb to make my body
porrsfow a gat dyet
duth for 4 dyes Shure
a dry. no pill but a pmge
Gate a pinge & newimg &
Gernshes ot & dyr.

GtWb g 7ʒ h: 3. 30 p m 1617

Anteony Nicolsmyall ese. Nowp 327
a bath ortWb 10 g h: 8. 45 cut m
1617

Vryn w ɛ tenth.
Sirk abdn afeutmys poh a ort 13. 30
gmy abunde ɛ smir fryrh gib 20. 9°
Wr vot take m shrin bot rusoth 16

muth:. dg: Simky Shuwlir muth
Symon nogshyn a an Eis sbufroh hoh gauth
his Gogs nowaign Goine Zborh an afe diar
afʒ hatgt rabwh iuar an Zij ay god Zij
fhogn nor gwly8o
a dyo8 diuh Sour Elij

yohy yohr eyzɲ num nub ho bloud ɛ ymr
bhuy tay Vonor ʒhyij
an Eiij fathinys
Eij thn ausd yo8 diuho
8ij nyuph fulemi Eiij

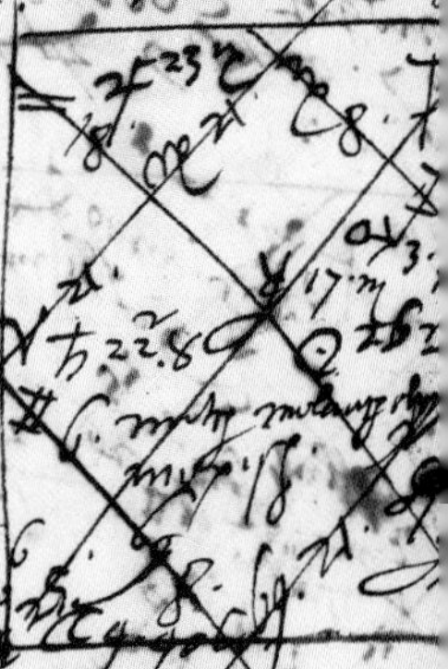

In different traditions, however, there are questions that cannot or should not be asked. This may be because of political or religious sensitivities (as in the cases mentioned earlier, it may be seen as treason to ask about the health of a king or queen or of a pope) or because they close down future possibilities (for example, Mambila diviners will not ask if someone will die). We have to keep in mind that there may be questions that are unaskable because they can't be framed as well as questions that, in principle, are askable but, in practice, are never asked. For each time and place we have to consider what the users of divination (both clients and diviners) consider to be good and bad questions to ask of divination. Such issues are affected by whether the divination system allows open-ended consultations ('How am I?') or whether only specific possibilities, with yes or no answers, rather than generalities can be asked.

Not only does the record often contain far more about the procedures used than the questions asked and the answers received, but we also know very little about what the clients did with the answers. Sometimes we know that clients thank the diviners politely and go away either to get another opinion or to do something other than what the diviner has suggested. In a few cases we may not know the question but the answer, or half an answer, may be enough to allow us to infer the question. Evidence for this has been found in ancient Greek shrines, where questions were written on lead sheets that have survived. However, there is a tantalising twist: the chosen alternatives would have been given to the clients to take away as evidence of the answer they had received. This means that what has survived are the alternatives *not* chosen by the oracle, in other words the answers that were rejected and thrown away. We are left to infer what

13 On 9 October 1617, the astrologer Richard Napier was visited by George Norris of Stevenage, a 32-year-old man who was 'crazed [in] his brayns for love to a wench', mopish and experiencing 'much melancholy'. Napier cast a horoscope and recommended bloodletting and purging.

the oracle actually chose, which is often unproblematic but sometimes impossible, such as with a choice between two names where we know only the person not chosen. Nonetheless, the scope of the binary choices is hugely revealing of how the clients understood the world they lived in.

It is now time to turn to the different types of divination explored in this book. In preparing it, we have struggled to find an auspicious order for the chapters that follow since there are so many rival possibilities: they could be arranged by geography or chronology to reveal useful contrasts by juxtaposing similar systems from different places or periods of history. In the end we did a bit of everything. We start with some of the oldest forms of divination and we end with the contemporary West. In between we have instances of astrology from different places and different times, contrasting examples that do similar things with cards, and quite different forms of divination such as Nuosu readings of patterns in egg whites or Tibetan rope divination. The best, most workable solutions are often not neat and tidy but uneasy mixtures, and no less auspicious for all that.

EXTISPICY IN ANCIENT MESOPOTAMIA

Parsa Daneshmand

Mesopotamian fortune telling is one of the oldest systems of divination for which we have records. In Mesopotamia, divination was a common way of making decisions and of gaining information about the past and future. The future was understood to consist of individual events, each of which was decided by the assembly of the gods. In the same vein, the past was a former future that had been decided by the gods, who were thus the authorities who could explain the reasons why past events had occurred. The gods always issued decisions in favour of or against the will of humans. Therefore, a question such as 'Should the king attack the enemy?' was considered a potential future, a case that should be decided. It was the gods who decided whether the king should attack or not. Divination as a ritual thus functioned to align human decisions with those of the assembly of the gods. As a part of decision-making processes, it was performed to consider different ideas for important decisions as the actual choice was made of which way to act. Ancient Mesopotamian divinatory texts indicate that diviners were required to provide firm answers from the gods to a broad range of questions regarding political and military decisions, including official appointments and warfare, as well as questions about natural disasters, family issues and health problems.

Extispicy, the act of observing the entrails of a sacrificed animal, including sheep and birds, was the most expensive Mesopotamian divinatory method (cheaper methods included oil and smoke divination). It was practised from the third millennium BCE onwards. By the second millennium BCE, it had become a high-prestige divinatory method for decision-making. Although most of the surviving divinatory texts deal with the observation of the liver of sheep, extispicy was by no means restricted to the inspection of livers, for other organs, such as the heart and lungs, were also studied. A later version practised by the Etruscans in northern Italy is usually called haruspicy.

In divination consultations, the human was the one who asked (*ša'ālu*) and the god the one who answered (*apālu*). A consultation was understood as a conversation between the gods and the client. The diviner acted only as an intermediary. The client had to be physically present in one form or another. However, clients could be animate or inanimate objects. For example, if the question was about a city, that city was the main client and the diviner was obliged to travel there to perform extispicy, or a lump of clay from that place (*kirbānu*) might instead be sent to the diviner as a proxy for the city. Similarly, if a

14 A cuneiform tablet containing an example of a bird divination consultation, c.200 BCE. This particular query, originating from Seleucid Uruk, was requested by Governor Anu-uballiṭ (known as *Kephalōn* in Greek). He was planning to decorate the statue of Ištar and thereby gain the goddess's favour.

consultation occurred in the absence of a person, some of their hair and a piece of their clothing (*šārtu u sissiktu*) had to be handed to the diviner for the ritual.

At the start of a consultation, the client's query was written on a clay tablet.[1] During the divination ritual, the tablet was placed on an altar dedicated to the god. An important step in divinatory consultation between the human and the gods was the offering of a sacrifice to the gods. After the animal was slaughtered by the diviner, the assembly of the gods would convene to discuss the matter. They would then convey their final decision through signs that were inscribed on the liver and other organs of the sacrificed animal. Diviners would observe the different omens and calculate an aggregate sum of the number of positive and negative signs. Mesopotamian diviners have provided long lists of good and bad signs, including their interpretation methods. In general, an animal organ that was healthy was usually a good omen.

After performing an extispicy, the diviner added a full description of the signs observed onto a part of the tablet that had been intentionally left blank. If there were more positive than negative signs the result was positive, and vice versa. If the positive and negative signs cancelled each other out, the result was uncertain and a check-up was required. There were two types of signs, including *pitruštu* (dark spots and splits) and *nipḫu* (some deformations) that could change the whole result, even if unfavourable signs were heavily outnumbered by favourable signs. In such a case, the diviner would recommend a follow-up consultation.

Two general questions could be posed through the practice of extispicy. The first regarded an individual's well-being, and the second the result of an action such as a battle. The surviving ancient Mesopotamian documents, however, mainly deal with real enquiries, where the question was more specific, for example, 'Should Assurbanipal, the crown prince of the Succession Palace, drink this herb, which is placed before your great divinity?' There were instances where the enquiries did not seek general advice but rather a specific outcome out of several possibilities. Questions such as 'Will this pregnant woman survive?' required explicit answers. Even in such cases the response provided could influence the choice between a magical or a medical course of action.

Extispicy provided binary answers – yes or no responses – to the most important decisions. In this divinatory system, there was, in general, no open-ended consultation. An answer such as 'You should go on campaign, but perhaps you should not' was contradictory and would not help the client. The clarity of divinatory advice in Mesopotamian consultations reflected the purpose of decision-making and indicates that divination in Mesopotamia was undertaken not to satisfy mere curiosity about future events but to transform a possibility into action.

The results of divinatory consultation were valid for only a limited period. This was called *adannu*. No situation would remain unchanged forever, and no diviner or adviser could guarantee the correctness of the outcome of divination for an unlimited or unspecified period of time. In addition, there were situations requiring immediate and urgent action. For instance, during an urgent threat posed by the Ben-Yaminites, an Amorite tribe targeting the valley of Terqa in early second millennium BCE Mesopotamia, an emissary of the king of Mari, facing this imminent danger, conducted a divination ritual to gather grain before the Ben-Yaminites could launch their attack. In a letter addressed to the

15 Clay model of a sheep's liver from 1900–1600 BCE that was probably used to instruct students in divination. The carved squares contain text explaining what the marks found on each segment of the organ indicate.

king of Mari, the agent reported: 'Regarding the harvest of the Terqa valley, I instructed the performance of an extispicy, and it yielded favorable outcomes for a span of three days.'[2]

In situations with lower risk, where there was not an immediate or actual threat, the time frame was extended further than it was in more urgent situations. For instance, when cities experienced relative safety and tranquillity without imminent threats from foreign or domestic adversaries, the usual duration of validity for an extispicy ensuring a city's safety would have been about a month. There was an inverse relationship between high-risk situations and the length of the time period for taking action.

ORACLES IN ANCIENT GREECE

Esther Eidinow

In the ancient world, across diverse cultures – from ancient Mesopotamia to Egypt, to Greece and to Rome – divination was a crucial resource that promised the possibility of finding out what was hidden. In these ancient cultures, gods and other supernatural forces were thought to be involved in planning human lives and also interfering in them, especially if a person had wronged someone else or had offended the gods. Surviving questions to the oracle of Zeus at Dodona in north-western Greece show how a community suffering from a natural disaster saw the event as divine punishment and consulted an oracle to find out what they had done to deserve it. One question, for example, was: 'The Dodonaeans ask Zeus and Dione whether it is because of the impurity of some man that god sends the storm?'

While the primary concern of individuals who used divination was to find out about the gods' plans regarding future events, divination was also practised to discover things that were hidden in the present or the past, such as where treasure was concealed, or the identity of thieves or those suspected of plotting or committing murder. For example, from the oracle of Zeus at Dodona, a question survives that asks: 'Did he

16 This early sixteenth-century engraving from *Master of the Die* (*c*.1530–60) depicts a consultation of the oracle of Apollo described in Ovid's fable of Cupid and Psyche.

[or she] introduce a poison [or potion] to my children or to my wife or to me [obtained] from Lyson?'

The processes of ancient divination may at first seem very varied. As mentioned in the Introduction, Cicero reported that, in the ancient world, divination techniques were divided into two sorts, which he called *technical* and *inspired*. The first category included seemingly purely mechanistic operations such as the choosing of lots or the throwing of dice, as well as forms that required technical knowledge, such as how to read the appearance of the livers of sacrificed animals. The second category consisted of inspired or enthusiastic divination, where a person became possessed by a god who then spoke through them. The most famous example of inspired divination was at Delphi, where a priestess called the Pythia became possessed by the god Apollo. While other forms of divination were sometimes doubted or even mocked in ancient texts, inspired divination seems to have been very highly respected in broader society.

We can trace the historical development of some of these practices. In ancient Mesopotamia, divination by means of omens could occur by means of events that were either unprovoked (naturally occurring, such as patterns of smoke) or provoked (through the sacrifice of animals as we saw in pp. 47–51). Within Mesopotamian culture, the former was very important, and there are large collections of clay tablets recording the meaning of many different kinds of such omens, from the shapes of mushrooms to the content of dreams, to the site of a city and to the presence of demons. While this omen practice died out early in Mesopotamian history, the reading of sacrifices became extremely important and influential throughout the ancient world. Babylonian divination techniques seem to have shaped Etruscan haruspicy (reading entrails, also called extispicy), which in turn were a part of Roman augury practices. We also see Babylonian influences in later Egyptian and Greek astrological activities.

In ancient Greece, many forms of divination took place at sacred sites, where a particular god or gods were worshipped. Some of these sites specialized in particular areas of concern. For example, the sanctuaries of the god Asklepios were focused on healing; these were incubation oracles, where visitors slept and dreamed the responses to their questions. Oracular sanctuaries could become very popular and prosperous. The oracular sanctuary of Apollo at Delphi was visited by people from all over the ancient world for over a thousand years, including important politicians asking questions about significant events. Visitors brought offerings to the god, both in advance of and after their consultations, and Delphi became extremely prosperous – but also gained a reputation for greed!

But there were also many smaller oracular sites, which were not as pricey or exclusive. For example, in the marketplace of the city of Pharae in Achaea, in southern Greece, there stood a statue of the god Hermes, with a small stone hearth in front of it decorated with bronze lamps, and an altar. To obtain a message from the gods, a person would burn incense in the hearth, fill and light the lamps, and make an offering of a local coin. They would then whisper their question in the statue's ear. The person would then leave, covering their ears so that they could not hear anything until they were outside the marketplace. Once they had removed their hands from their ears, they would treat the first thing they heard as the divine answer to their question.

Those who could not visit an oracular site might instead consult an itinerant *mantis*, or 'seer', who would

following pages

17 Camillo Miola's painting *The Oracle* (1880) depicts the famous Delphic oracle. Here a priestess called the Pythia, sitting on a tripod, has become possessed by Apollo and is in the middle of delivering a message to a client.

travel from community to community, selling their skills in reading omens or sacrifices. Most of these travelling seers were male, but there is evidence that some women took on these roles. Alternatively, one might buy a reading from a travelling *chresmologos*, an 'oracle-speaker' or '-collector'. Such individuals carried collections of oracular sayings, often consisting of single statements or verses from ancient poetry; for a fee, they would identify which of these sayings offered the 'right' answer to one's question.

One such collection that survives, the *Sortes Astrampsychi*, probably originally dates back to between the first century BCE and 236 CE, although the eleven papyri on which it survives date from a later period. The user selected a question closest to their own concern (e.g., 'Will I marry and will it be to my advantage?', 'Will I profit from the undertaking?'), and then, through a series of calculations ('choose a random number between one and ten'), would be directed to an answer. Useful responses were concealed among numerous fake answers. The *Sortes Astrampsychi* includes questions that are obviously asked by enslaved people ('Will I be freed from servitude?', 'Am I going to be sold?'). They are further evidence that in the ancient world people from all social levels regarded divination as an important tool for decision-making.

18 A fragment of the *Sortes Astrampsychi*, an ancient papyrus recording a set of oracular questions (e.g., 'Am I to recover from my illness?', 'Am I to be separated from my wife?') and possible answers, which are reached by following a series of calculations.

ANCIENT JEWISH BIBLIOMANCY

Pieter W. van der Horst

Soon after the books of the Jewish Bible (the Hebrew Bible or Old Testament) had for the most part been completed in the third century BCE, they gradually gained canonical and authoritative status among the Jews. This almost inevitably led to these books being regarded as holy writings of divine origin. As such, they were viewed as the repository of divine wisdom and hence of God's knowledge – not only of the past but also of the present and the future. It was not long before the Hebrew Bible began to be used as a collection of divine oracles that could be consulted for advice and help in various circumstances.

In Hebrew culture, bibliomancy, or *Sortes Biblicae*, is the practice of using biblical texts to get to know what God has in store for individuals or groups, not by reading the biblical text but by using it as a lot oracle. One of the earliest Jewish examples of this practice comes from the First Book of Maccabees, composed in the late second century BCE. The book tells the story of military commanders who, prior to a decisive battle, unrolled the Torah scroll at random in the hope that the first line their eyes lit upon would instruct them about what God had in store for them or expected them to do. The Second Book of Maccabees describes the same story, explaining that

19 An eighteenth-century engraving from Jan Luyken's *La voix de Dieu par l'urim & le thummim* (1705) depicting the use of the Urim and Tummin, an oracular device mentioned in Exodus 28:30 and 1 Samuel. These texts describe the device as being worn on the breastplate of the high priest.

Judas the Maccabee read 'the help of God' in the text, and took this as a sign to proceed with the battle (which they won).

What had been the role of a prophet in former times had now been taken over by the biblical text. Whereas in previous centuries, it was the prophets or an oracular device called the Urim and Tummim (probably sacred dice with yes and no answers) to which the Israelites turned to consult God, in the Hellenistic period it was the divinely inspired books that were increasingly regarded as the storehouse of all wisdom. The procedure of opening a biblical book at random in search of advice or help has remained in use up to the present day among certain Christian and Muslim groups.

In the Middle Ages, specific manuals of lot oracles (*goralot*) also developed in Jewish culture, although there is some evidence that these texts date back to late antiquity. These books were intended to give users insight into their future or into matters hidden from natural perception, but also counsel in making decisions in difficult situations. At their simplest the manuals contained lists of answers that were vague enough for them to be linked to whatever question the enquirer posed. Later manuals also included lists of questions and more complex methods for using the biblical text to select from the list of answers. In this system, the biblical word or passage thus found was not meant to be the answer itself but instead was to be used to find the right number in the list of solutions. Here too it was assumed that God guided the whole procedure to obtain the desired answer.

Goralot books suggest that lot divination involved both a client (the questioner) and an expert diviner. The questions posed could vary from enquiries about travel to business, family life and similar everyday themes.

20 A fifteenth-century *Sefer ha-Goralot* (*Book of Lots*), used in Jewish culture in seeking answers to difficult questions.

תמים תהיה עם ה' אלהיך · אחרי · שמעו אלי ונו'

הרוצה לחשוב בעולות או יחפץ בלשון הצאות על האלה אשר הוא שגל
וידוע ובעימצאה · יכל העולות בקובייאות ביו ובן חברי
נשעני · וילול לעורס ויעלוך מפרס אם נשאר ביו כתר עיב ישמור
מפטר היורך אויקור על הקטף · או על עודי קנודת ויעלול מפרס ס
ועלוך עד שאר ביו כתר עיב · וישמור המפכר אשר נשאר ויא על האלה
אשר לרס וישוב מתני ועומא צאה על האלה עד שיצא המפטר אשר
ביו וישמור האלה אשר יצלה כה הוכפר וידעתי זה פרטני יט · ואם ס
שלימתו האלה הכתובת בלום ולא יצלה המשכן שוב לחשוב עומא הלח
ומקום שיצלה המשכן ידע הפרטני אשר כעבו ויביון עלו בלום והפדתנו
ההוא שלמיון חל התלך אשר היה הפרטני ההוא מעול שלו בעלותו · וימלך
ההוא יבריק בעת התולבס והוא שנבנד אל הבהמה ואחל ההיה אשר תהת
ידו אשר עמונה הקבל הוה לעשות וערי העולך לבריק בעת התריק · או
הבהמות והיא העדיעני העוף אשר יהיה חנב על דבר שאתי ויצא לאור
השוך ההוא ויחשוב מפטר קשאר ביו אתר שמי · ויצא נט העשן · ההוא
השובה שאתה אם עוב אם רע קנט · וזאת המחבר עלו ואלא שלא

על צה שלא כנוה אם זא לשמוע · מהם קשובה נכוה ולויות
ויתב שהתב צהה עותהעבוע חייו מועא שבן שאיון ולכן צה שלא יביון
צהה כי אם תלב עתבנו · וכן צה שלא יבין צהה כי אם צלולך שובת ולא פוס
שובך לא תיכבך חיתיר והיה שלא מתב שעולצו צהה מול יתאריס ולא יבין
כהס לא פוס בעולה צללך ולא נשעה ונבשעולשות כהם מול תאריס כבן ד
רבעתך עליות שין ושעה אתרנה חייס יבעע ושתיה יולוס חתיש · וצאה
ויוס אצי · כל תעשה הלא חייס ראיוס להעלבס עעלוי · וכן יוס
מועל החדש ויוס שלבתו ויוס שלאתרין הרי ניתיס נכן הבה מעולת
על עבקי · העולת על רעת חיוי הכותבס והם שלתיס אל התולבס מתב
שבע אלה מבנס דיק הקתמות · ומחו שהנצחיס שלתי היקוס
נכל חבונ שאתהתחד ונבעולה כתוב כ לא יעשה · שעתייס דבר כ אם
נטה סורו אלועבדיו העשאיס ·

The manuals stress that the questions posed should be serious, not frivolous, and the answers too were taken seriously by the enquirer. Anyone who tries to test the lot oracle, or who scoffs at it, will not receive a correct answer. These books continue to circulate among ultra-orthodox Jewish groups today.

In the rabbinic literature of the Roman and early Byzantine period, there was also widespread use of cledonomancy (prognostication or divination through the interpretation of chance encounters), using the utterances of schoolchildren about a biblical text. In antiquity there was a widespread assumption that children possessed the gift of prophecy. In the Babylonian Talmud, a rabbi wanted to know whether it was a good idea to make a visit to a colleague in Babylon. To make sure that this was the right decision, he asked a child, 'What is the last biblical verse you learned?' The answer that was given was 1 Samuel 28:3: 'Now Samuel was dead.' Even though this was said about the biblical prophet Samuel, it was clear to the rabbi that it was not a good idea for him to make the trip.

Here it is not a matter of opening the Holy Book at random but of a random questioning of children in the expectation that the first biblical verse they quote contains God's message for a particular situation. But the principle is the same: since all that God has said and will continue to say to humans is contained in the Torah, and since God can be trusted to guide and control the process of consultation, the answer is incontrovertible. As Ben Bag-Bag, an early rabbi, is reported to have said about the Torah, 'Turn it, and turn it again [i.e., study it from every angle], for everything is in it' (Pirkei Avot 5:22) – not only everything of the past, but also of the present and future.

MESOAMERICAN DIVINATION

Alessia Frassani

Indigenous communities in Mexico and Guatemala today make use of a number of divinatory techniques to help those who might visit a diviner seeking clarity on personal issues, social conflicts or health concerns. Divination in Mesoamerica changed dramatically with the Spanish invasion, but the survival of centuries-old divination codices can provide us with rich insights into these long-standing traditions. While making inferences about historical practices from contemporary activity is fraught with difficulty, studying the surviving sources alongside religious practices in modern Indigenous communities allows us to speculate and perhaps recover something about pre-Columbian practices.

The most common Spanish term for a diviner is *curandero* (healer), a reference to their ability to address physical illness as well as personal and sometimes rather mundane problems. *Curanderos* can be male or female. The most common ceremonial items found in a *curandero*'s house are a table or altar, on which images of Catholic saints have now replaced Mesoamerican gods. Before colonization, the ritual area was a straw mat on the floor. The mats then, and altars now, are usually oriented towards the east and the rising sun. Flowers and leaves are kept on the altar to ritually cleanse the client either in preparation for or following the consultation. Similarly, the altar table is covered with a white cloth, signalling its purity and the clarity that derives from the place to the east where knowledge resides.

Sixteenth-century ethnograhic accounts show that, since pre-Columbian times in Mesoamerica, as in modern Indigenous Mexico and Guatemala, queries regarding the nature of physical pain or interpersonal conflict have usually been answered through the interpretation of a handful of maize kernels, dried beans or seeds that the diviner casts onto the altar table. The positions and shapes of the grains lead to different interpretations; for example, a maize grain that falls on its embryonic side (whence it would sprout) is positive and alive, while one that falls on the other side is considered dead. Also, if a kernel points towards the others at the centre of the table, it is considered positive and a sign of abundance, while if a kernel falls far away from the others and points outwards it is considered a waste of wealth and resources. Kernels that fall on top of each other indicate conflict and possibly infidelity in marriage.

Further techniques can be documented in modern times. For example, an egg may also be used, where the diviner cracks open the egg and pours it into a glass of water: the shape, colour and consistency of the yolk and albumen provide important clues for the reading. The flickering flame and dripping wax of a candle can also be consulted by the *curandero* on request. Other essential elements employed during divinatory sessions are wild tobacco, used to rub the patient's arms, as well as incense that is burned with wood in a brazier. Both actions are meant to give strength to the patient.

Ancient divinatory manuscripts, known today only through a few surviving examples, report indirectly on

21 In pre-Columbian Mesoamerica, the success of a marriage could be forecast by making calculations based on a couple's calendrical names, as pictured here in Codex Laud, which probably dates from the fifteenth century.

similar practices. The manuscripts themselves were yet
another instrument used by the priest during their mantic
and ceremonial activities. The writing on these leather
folded books is pictorial and depicts animals, gods or
people engaged in rituals with the use of plants or other
ceremonial objects.

As these manuscripts show, ancient Mesoamerican
religious books were principally organized according to
the calendar. The wider importance of the calendar can
be seen in the way people were usually named for the day
on which they were born. Fig. 21 shows several marriage
prognostications based on the sum of the numerals of the
couple's calendrical names. Still in use in some parts of

southern Mexico and Guatemala, the 260-day calendar is derived from the unique combination of thirteen numerals and twenty day signs. Besides thirteen and twenty, periods of five and four days are especially important for divination.

In its contemporary form the most common result of these consultations is that the client makes an offering in a designated place. This is often in their garden at home, but sometimes takes place in more remote places such as caves or mountain tops. Offerings are made either to strengthen the place where the patient lives, so that bad influences do not affect them, or to restore a positive relationship with a god in case they have offended them. The offering may consist of eggs, candles, cacao beans, feathers, incense, wild tobacco and other objects that the *curandero* prepares in paper bundles. Fig. 22, for example, shows a young woman extinguishing the flames of a bundle of burning pine sticks, an action that would now normally be conducted by a client on the priest's instruction. The eight dots and the symbol for water on top indicate the best moment to undertake the ritual action according to the Mesoamerican calendar, known as *tonalpohualli* (meaning 'count of days' in Nahuatl, the language of the Aztecs). The lower part of the manuscript shows offerings of pine stick bundles, egg albumen, a coral branch and a cut flower. The vertical black lines show the correct position and number of the offerings (each bar indicates a group of five items).

Another facet of Mesoamerican divination found in both ancient books and modern practices are night ceremonies, sometimes referred to as *veladas* (vigils). These are carried out under the guidance of a priest with the intent of gaining clarity on one's condition, the future and actions that need to be taken to achieve a desired outcome. Participants of night ceremonies consume sacred plants

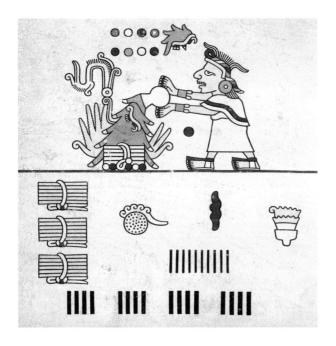

and use techniques such as repeated chanting to alter their state of consciousness. Through these methods, the client and the priest (or guide) are able to connect with the ancestors and other supernatural beings, who will instruct them on the path to be taken. Before colonization, an encounter with a deified ancestor usually took place in a temple especially with regard to important political decisions. Historical events narrated in Mixtec genealogical manuscripts, for example, refer to the momentous visit to the Death Temple, or the Vehe Kihin (Great Temple), in Mixtec, on the part of local leaders. Today night ceremonies are normally conducted in the *curandero*'s home and almost exclusively for the sake of the client's health.

22 A young woman, possibly a priestess, extinguishes the flames of a bundle of burning pine sticks as part of a divination ritual.

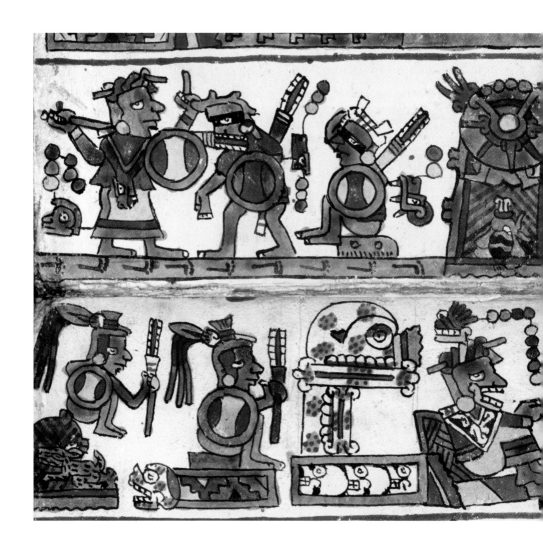

23 This section of the Codex Añute (c.1541) may depict a night ceremony. It is read from right to left in the bottom row and from left to right in the top row. Lady 6 Monkey encounters Lady 9 Grass, guardian of the Death Temple, the Sacred Place of the Ancestors, to make a decision regarding war and dynastic succession. As a result, Lady 6 Monkey wages war against two enemies, one of whom is eventually sacrificed.

القول على الاقليم الثاني للمشتري

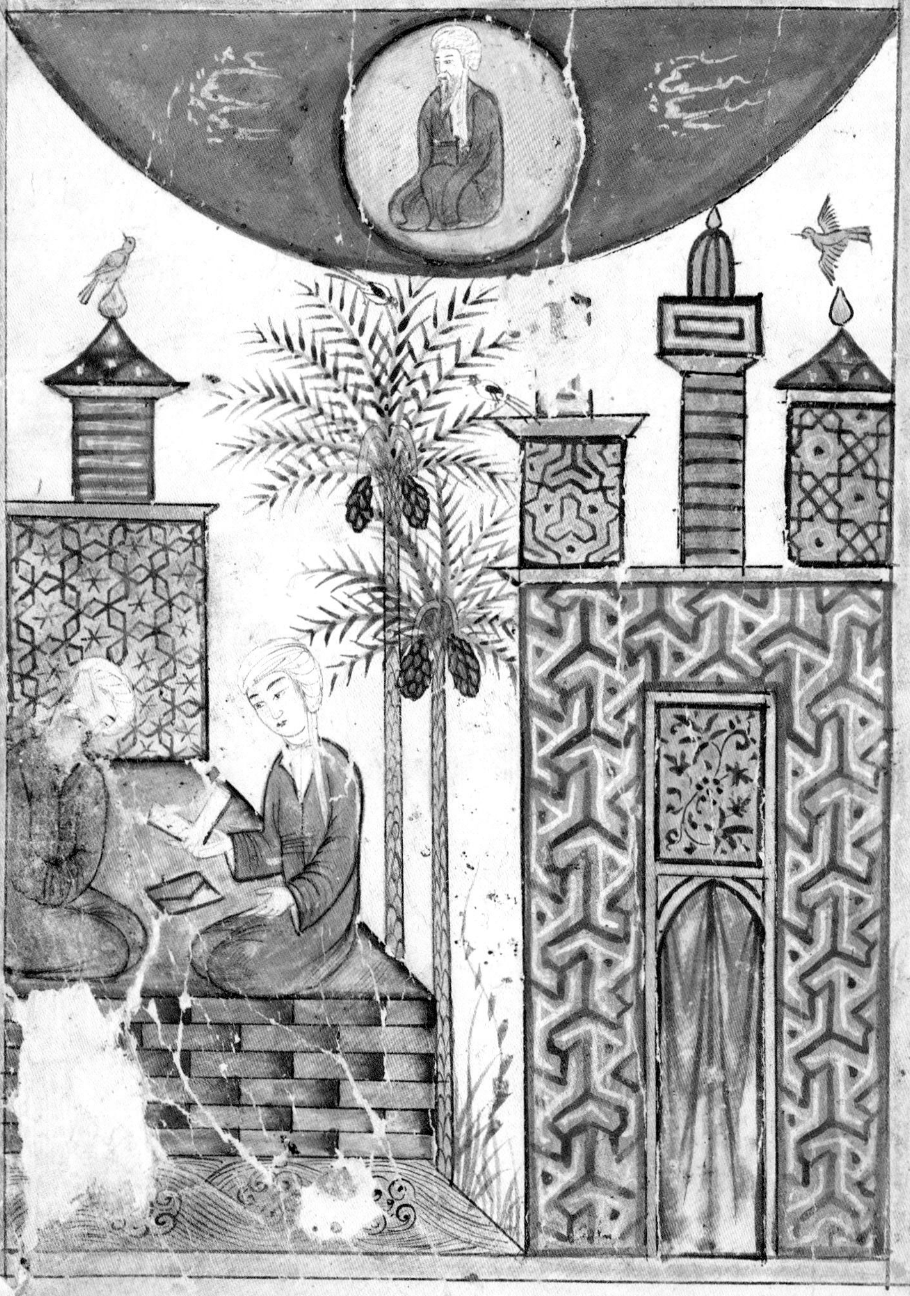

OTTOMAN ASTROLOGY

A. Tunç Şen

As in many other medieval and early modern cultures, astrology was a widely practised form of divination in the Ottoman world, both in a courtly context and among the broader public. More documentary evidence is available about the former, thanks to the institutionalization of astrological practice at the Ottoman court as an office led by the chief astrologer (*munajjimbashi*) and staffed by his associates. This position, which appeared in bureaucratic registers by the second half of the fifteenth century, remained intact until the official demise of the Ottoman Empire after the First World War. One of the most resilient administrative units in the long history of the empire, the office of the chief court astrologer was tasked with presenting annual almanacs with prognostications (*taqwīm*), preparing birth horoscopes (particularly for members of the ruling dynasty), delivering short memos to designate astrologically auspicious moments before the initiation of imperial enterprises such as military campaigns or the construction of colossal buildings, and providing astrological commentary, either verbally or in writing, at the time of celestial oddities.

The rich textual corpus this office left behind shows that different branches and genres of astrology were in regular use in the Ottoman world. These include

24 The *Kitāb al-Bulhān* (*Book of Wonders*) is a collection of divinatory works dating back to the late fourteenth century. This page illustrates the Ptolemaic theory of the seven climes that make up the earth. The second clime is associated with Jupiter, which is itself associated with intellectual pursuits, reflected here in the depiction of two learned individuals.

genethlialogy, or natal astrology, which deals specifically with interpreting the celestial configuration at the moment of an individual's birth; electional astrology, which is concerned with designating the most favourable moment for undertaking a particular activity; and horary astrology or interrogations, which seeks to answer a client's question by interpreting a horoscope cast at the time the question is posed. Each of these distinct branches of astrology required the Ottoman astrologer to calculate the planetary positions for the moment in question (whether it be the time of birth, the solar equinox and the beginning of the new solar year or the time when a client asked their question). The practitioner then interpreted that celestial configuration according to a set of theories.

Precise astronomical computations were essential for providing accurate astrological advice, and so Ottoman astrologers relied on different sets of instruments, from books to astronomical instruments such as astrolabes and quadrants. The fundamental textual tool of Ottoman astrologers was the astronomical handbooks of tables (*zīj*), which presented all the data and parameters astrologers needed for computing planetary movements and positions. These tables were compiled by dint of systematic celestial observations conducted at observatories founded at different periods of Islamic history and in diverse regions. The two tables in wide circulation among fifteenth- and sixteenth-century Ottoman astrologers were the Ilkhanid tables (*Zīj-i Ilkhānī*), prepared at the Maragha observatory in the thirteenth century by the famous Persian polymath Nasir al-Din al-Tusi and his associates, and the Ulugh Beg tables (*Zīj-i Sulṭānī*), composed by astronomers and mathematicians convened at the Samarqand observatory in the fifteenth century by the Timurid prince Ulugh Beg. From the seventeenth century onwards, Ottoman astrologers began to engage more with state-of-the-art astronomical tables produced in Europe, including the *Tables astronomiques* (1740) by Jacques Cassini.

Fifteenth- and sixteenth-century Ottoman astrologers, however, often encountered inconsistencies between the predicted timing of celestial phenomena (such as eclipses or conjunctions) according to these tables, and the actual time they occurred based on their own observations. These discrepancies prompted several Ottoman astral experts in the sixteenth century to demand additional royal support for constructing an observatory that would improve the data and parameters in the existing tables. An observatory was eventually established in the late sixteenth century by the chief astrologer, but it functioned for only a few years and was eventually destroyed as a result of the political and religious authorities' growing unease about the observatory and the activities of the astrologer.

As this demonstrates, Ottoman astral experts, much like their counterparts in other cultures, operated within a social, cultural and epistemic order where their expertise was frequently called into question, regardless of how much the ruling elites made use of their services. Although in the Ottoman context there was no equivalent disciplinary mechanism to the Inquisition in Catholic Europe, multiple actors from diverse social backgrounds – including religious scholars (*ulama*), mystics (*Sufis*) and authors of ethical treatises – often raised concerns about astrologers and their practice. Furthermore, the standard institute of higher education in the Ottoman context, the *madrasa*, did not promote the study of books and sciences related

to astrological practice. In the relative absence of an institutional framework where astral sciences were taught and transmitted, aspiring astrologers acquired their knowledge through master–apprentice relationships established either in the relevant office at the imperial court or in other informal social networks.

In addition to the more technical and mathematical form of astrological practice undertaken in the Ottoman imperial court, another kind of astrology was also sought after by laypeople. Unlike the practice of learned astrology, which required the tedious calculation of celestial positions and variables based on the exact time and location of the astrological matter in question, lay astrology did not involve such mathematical sophistication and astronomical rigor. Instead, practitioners of lay astrology often replaced detailed scientific calculations with either folk knowledge about the cyclical patterns of celestial occurrences or with esoteric and often simplistic numerological explanations ascribed to celestial objects. The basic idea behind the latter was to establish an interpretive framework of correspondences between the numerological values of names, the seven planets, the twelve zodiac signs, the twenty-eight lunar mansions and other heavenly bodies, all of which were designed by God and operated through the mediation of spirits, angels and hidden saints.

Whether it was the learned version of erudite astrologers or the lay method that lacked mathematical refinement, astrological practice in the Ottoman world was predicated on the fundamental Hermetic principle that terrestrial occurrences are necessarily linked to the celestial world.

25 The sign of Cancer (or *al-Saratān*) is here depicted in the *Kitāb al-Bulhān* (*Book of Wonders*). Cancer is shown here with its ruling planet, the Moon. Venus, Mercury and the Moon, the three decans of Cancer, are depicted from right to left at the bottom of the page.

following pages

26 The sign of Cancer depicted in Abd al-Rahman al-Sufi's highly influential *Kitāb suwar al-kawākib* (*Book of Fixed Stars*), written around 964 CE. This copy was made in Iraq in 1170.

حد ولكوكبه السرطان زبراله ت مٮ على ما ٮ المجسطى و الطول

أسمآ الَكوَاكب

العرض			الطول			اسماء الكواكب	
ٮ	م	٥	لح	٥	نح	الوسطى من الاسماك السحابى الدى فى الصدره ٮعال المعلف	١
د	ا	٥	كز	٥	نه	السحابى من الاسل المقدم من زى الاربعه الاصلاح الدرجول	ٮ
د	ٮ	٥	كح	٥	نه	الجنوبى من الاسل المقدم	ج
د	و	٥	لح	٥	نه	السحابى من الاسل الما ٮمن زى الاربعه الاصلاح المٮٮربعالعا	د
د	ٮ	٥	كد	٥	نه	اميلاهدرس الى الجنوب	ه
ٮ	ا	٥	كط	٥	نس	الدى على الراما الجنوبى	و
ٮ	ا	٥	كا	٥	نه	الدى على الراما الشمالى	ز
ٮ	ا	م	نه	٥	نه	الدى على الرجل الموجه الشمالى	ح
د	ا	٥	كد	٥	نه	الدى على الرجل الموجه الجنوبى	ط

وبلط كواكب منها مرالبرر الرابع ٮ وه الخامس ا وسحابى
الدى حول الصوره ولمسه صوره السرطان

						اسماء الكواكب	
كا	ٮ	د	ٮ	د	ٮ	الدى وٯ المرو الراما الجنوبى	ا
م	ٮ	د	٥	د	ٮ	المالى للطرف الراما الجنوبى	ٮ
د	ٮ	٥	كو	٥	نح	المقدم من الاسل الما العالارس وٯ السحابى	ح
ٮ	ٮ	٥	كط	٥	نح	المالى منها	١

وبلط د كواكب منها مرالعدرالرابع ٮٮ وفى الخامس ٮ

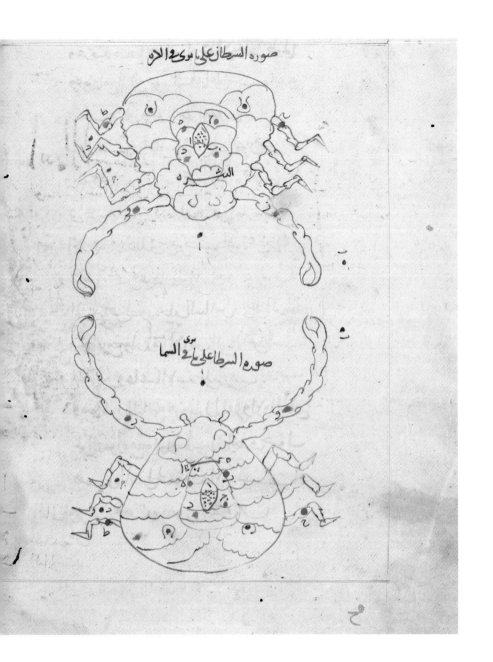

صوره السرطان علي مري في الارض

الشرطه

صوره السرطان علي مري في السما

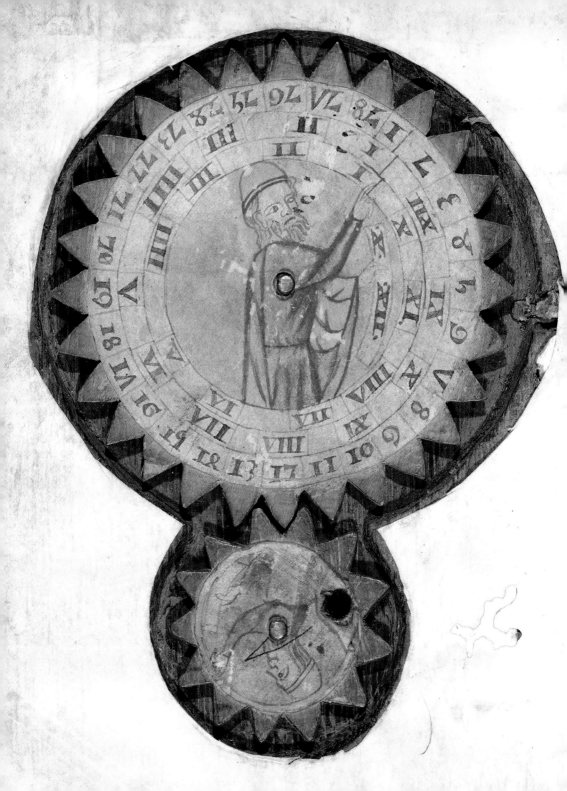

SORTILEGE IN MEDIEVAL EUROPE

Sophie Page

In the Middle Ages in Europe, if you had a difficult question you might seek the answer in a *Sortes*, or lot book. These medieval books of fate used random choice mechanisms such as the roll of a dice or the spin of a rotatable parchment disc. The more complex *Sortes* offered 144 possible responses to twelve set questions relating to the challenges of everyday life that could be applied to more specific questions such as how to achieve a healthy body, an advantageous marriage or a large inheritance, or how to avoid one's enemies, theft or imprisonment. *Sortes* originated in a vibrant Mediterranean culture of Greek, Arabic, Hebrew and Latin divination. At least nineteen different kinds of *Sortes* texts circulated in medieval Europe, and they were popular in several languages and different formats in the fourteenth and fifteenth centuries.

Sortes are simple to use and demand no external knowledge or expertise. A common format provides a list of questions, each linked to an illustration of an oracle called a judge (typically a saint, a king, a philosopher or an animal). For example, if you wanted to know whether a pregnant woman would have a boy or girl, or whether a lost item would be recovered, you would use the random choice mechanism to select a number (usually from two

27 A volvelle made of wood has been pasted into a carved slot in the binding of this late fourteenth-century English collection of fortune-telling tracts. Spinning the cogwheels allowed a key number to be identified that would then be located in the tables of the manuscript to find the answer to one's question.

to nine) and leaf through the manuscript to find the judge (one of twelve saints, kings, philosophers or animals) that corresponds to your question. Then you would consult the numbered answer attached to that judge. The written answers are rendered evocative by the visual charm of the illustrated book and intimate by their use of the second person singular.

A *Sortes* could be a self-help guide, but in a more formal ritual a client (*cliens*) or questioner (*quaerens*) might consult a *sortilegus*, who owned the book and would speak in the role of the judge. *Sortes* had their origins in ancient oracles but also referred to biblical prophecy or visions. After the translating movement of the twelfth and thirteenth centuries introduced Arabic texts to the Latin West, astrology became more prestigious, and planetary or zodiac sign judges increased in popularity. Towards the end of the Middle Ages, *Sortes* assumed the character of a light-hearted game, more playful than portentous, with bird, bat and butterfly judges as popular as the philosophers 'Socrates' and 'Cicero'.

Alongside this general evolution of style, individual *Sortes* were adapted to the interests or anxieties of their users. Some texts were highly Christianized, reassuring their users of the piety of their divining activities by combining the random process with prayers, fasting and the offering of alms. Other *Sortes* appealed to more scientific enthusiasms, instructing their users to calculate favourable celestial conditions before asking questions. Judges in the first kind of books might be saints, prophets or bishops; those in the second, philosophers or planets. For medieval enthusiasts of divination, religion and science were not, of course, mutually exclusive. Many single volumes contain both types of *Sortes* (for example, Fig. 28 shows a divinatory handbook copied

28 A page from a divinatory handbook compiled *c*.1250 by the monk Matthew of Paris. This page depicts the *spera volatilium*, one of thirteen redirecting circles, each with specific themes, that direct the client to the judge for their question.

Opera Volatilium

Valadrius fiait dicit phifiologus toc'

and illustrated by the monk Matthew of Paris around 1250).

Medieval people were just as anxious about the future as we are. *Sortes* borrowed the framework of Christian rituals and astrological techniques to seem less like an arbitrary, random process and more like a ritual space in which a solution was provided by divine will or planetary influence. But why were animals like birds, bats and butterflies considered as suitable as bishops and philosophers for answering questions about the challenges of human life? The answer is that animals were important spiritual symbols, and nature was a book whose secrets could be understood by the wise. Broadly, this emphasis on the goodness of God's creation was a response to mainstream Christian anxiety about dualist heresies and its negative perceptions of bodies and matter.

Of the thirty-six judges in the *Prenostica Pitagorice consideracionis*, the bee, locust and grasshopper feature alongside more typical prophetic birds such as the owl, raven and swallow and several lost and garbled species unknown to Latin translators of the original Hebrew text. Birds are frequently found in *Sortes*, being suited to the divinatory process because (according to mocking sceptics) their flight, chatter, caws and song were often mistaken for omens. One of the most significant portents was the caladrius, a rare white bird from Persia that was

29 In this illuminated thirteenth-century bestiary (book of beasts), a caladrius turns its back on a mortally sick king.

said to be able to cure a sick person by taking on their infection and flying towards the sun to burn up the infectious vapours. As Fig. 29 shows, the caladrius's gaze could reveal the fate of invalids. If the bird turned to face them they would be cured, but if it turned away they would die.

More prosaically, the twelfth-century English cleric John of Salisbury recommended observing the gull, kingfisher and swan because their nest building is a sign of imminent warmer weather, a kind of forecasting he thought would be particularly helpful to sailors. If one sees a duck diving joyfully, John explained, one can expect showers, not because the duck has a divine nature or knowledge of the future but because it is at home in the air and sensitive to changes in the atmosphere, which cause it joy or fear in anticipation of changing weather. John had little patience for augury, feeling that soon enough everything in the world will have some significance and we will be afraid to step out of our homes. His response to those who asked which prophetic birds can reveal the secrets of the future is the sarcastic remark 'Why, surely, they are those who were once human and who the ancient poets tell us were turned into birds'. Yet the birds in the *Sortes* support this joke, as they anthropomorphically advise, chide and offer solutions to their questioners. 'O human' they begin, and although their answers might sometimes be negative (e.g., 'What you seek will not be in your power') they tend towards the cautiously optimistic, giving hope in a characteristically vague way: 'So too in a short while will your mind return to brightness from the point where you seem to be in doubt. And it will come to you, and you will obtain what you desire with God's help. After the sun, the stars come out.'[1]

NECROMANCY IN MEDIEVAL EUROPE

Sophie Page

Necromancers – medieval Christian demon conjurors – thought that they could compel demons to reveal the truth about anything they asked, including all the secrets of the past, present and future. Demons had access to extraordinary knowledge because of their immortality and superior rationality. It was not that they were omniscient but rather that they had lived for a very long time, had seen it all before and were superlative predicters. Some medieval thinkers thought of demons as the first natural scientists, permitted by God to pass the aeons observing and interpreting humans to puzzle out each sin an individual was likely to succumb to. As the demons wandered eternally in the sublunar realm, they noticed things of great interest to the necromancer, such as where treasure was buried, who had stolen objects of value, who was an unfaithful lover, who had been wrongfully imprisoned and the guilty secrets of princes. Despite the intense malice and cunning of demons, medieval necromancers thought (or hoped) that their own faith, clerical office, ascetic practices and careful performance of the necromantic ritual would compel the demons to make truthful revelations of hidden things.

How did their rituals work? The necromancer could choose to work alone (sometimes accompanied by a

30 A sixteenth-century magic mirror associated with the demon (or fallen angel) Floren, or Floron. The demon assumed the shape of an armed knight sitting on a horse and was summoned into the mirror to answer questions about the past, present and future.

dog to intimidate the demons) or with a small number of companions. He (the necromancer is almost always a cleric) needed to own, borrow or commission a book that described essential ritual formulae and images, and optional instruments to add vivid theatricality such as a wand, a pentagram, a bell or special clothing. Next, he selected a space to work, perhaps their own bedroom or isolated woods. Timing was also important: it usually related planetary movements to the goal of the operation. For example, Saturn's associations with old age, wealth and violence made the hours or days it ruled over particularly suitable for experiments to identify a thief or find hidden treasure.

The necromancer made careful preparations to protect himself from demonic malice. He might draw and step inside a protective magic circle, summon the demon onto a small lead plate called a lamina (thereby reducing the spirit to a harmless size), or interact through a safe medium (a mirror worked well). Often, he would carry a sword. A spirit might be further mollified by the sacrifice of an animal, such as a bat, cat or hoopoe bird. Many experiments required a child intermediary, whose innocence was a defence against injury and whose pure gaze saw through obfuscation.

At the heart of these rituals was the invocation of demons. They were usually commanded by the powers of heaven and earth, above all by God the creator, to fulfil the will of the necromancer, who would engage with God and the spirits in a variety of registers from persuasive to threatening, through liturgy, prayer, conjuration or exorcism. Once present, the spirit was commanded to truthfully give the desired knowledge to the necromancer. When this had been achieved, it was ordered to leave at once and without violence.

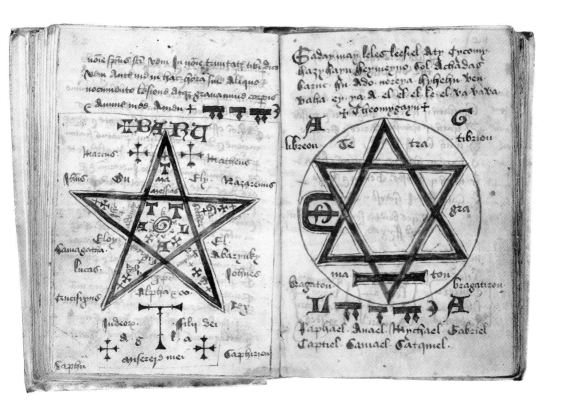

Necromantic rituals are often called *experimenta* in manuscripts, a term evocative of an operation to achieve a specific goal that has been tested to prove that it works. Like most medieval magic rituals, necromantic experiments were constantly varied in the search for improvement – for better results or protection from harm, or as a cosmological adaptation to fit the practitioner's world view. A new user of the necromantic handbook depicted in Fig. 31, for example, might avoid experiments using animal sacrifices (too distasteful) or angels (unlikely to help uncover theft) but be attracted to

31 A fifteenth-century Latin and Middle English necromantic handbook depicting sigils and pentagrams.

a ritual that restrained a demon with various astrological strategies, if belief in celestial influences was important to them. Essentially these are do-it-yourself rituals that contain a few fixed and many adjustable elements.

The late medieval universe of spirits was a syncretic but veiled realm. Although nominally divided between the clear categories of good angels and evil demons, it was also the product of a Christian tendency to absorb other religions' deities and spirits – whether Greek and Roman gods, Arabic djinn, Indigenous fairies, Jewish angels or Greek *daimones*. Aiding this absorption was a lack of named individual spirits among the heavenly throngs (except for the Devil and a few archangels), a result of early medieval anxiety that cults of angels would diminish the majesty of God.

The mystery and ambiguity of the spirit realm presented serious danger to Christians because evil spirits were thought to mimic the characteristics of angels to trap unwitting Christian souls. Necromancy used orthodox protective measures and rituals, such as the invocation of God, fasting and holy oil. This unsettles attempts to unpack the mentality of its practitioners. On the one hand, necromantic rituals clearly express the medieval longing for spiritual experiences and the self-assurance that holiness would overcome evil. On the other, intense engagement with demons suggests an acutely transgressive ritual performed by clerics who were disaffected with mainstream religion.

But perhaps more important than the motivation of either rebellion against religious norms or pious domination over evil is that the most common goal of divinatory necromantic rituals was to detect a thief. As well as speaking to a pragmatic and likely pecuniary necromancer–client relationship, this reflects the idea

that an evil spirit was particularly useful for tracking
down the sinful. Handbooks admitted, however, that
demons couldn't provide information about penitent
thieves if they had attended mass, confessed to a priest
or given the proceeds of their theft to the poor.

Many Christians thought that the whole moral
edifice of necromancy – a good Christian claiming to
be acting as an instrument of God while commanding
evil demons to do his will – was the delusion of a 'cursed
imagination' (as the fifteenth-century author John
Lydgate put it). Whether cursed or not, imagination
was central to necromancy and part of its appeal.

32 The Pilgrim meeting the
messenger of Necromancy,
from John Lydgate's *The
Pilgrimage of the Life of Man*
(fifteenth century).

A seventeenth-century depiction of the witch of Endor using a spirit to contact the dead King Samuel, as described in the book of 1 Samuel (*Sadducismus triumphatus*, 1681).

Many divinatory experiments were intended to locate hidden treasure, as part of a fantasy world of flying horses, illusory castles, bewitched thieves and revealed secrets that suggests that the authors of necromantic handbooks were steeped in literary romances as well as in the rituals of Christian liturgy.

JEWISH DREAM DIVINATION

Alessia Bellusci

In their long global history, Jews have developed, adopted and used many forms of divination including astrology, physiognomy, palmistry, geomancy and bibliomancy. Among Jews, dream divination occupies a special place. Premodern Jews held dreams in high regard, believing them to be close to prophecy or even to be a minor form of prophecy. The many accounts of dreaming and dreams in the Hebrew Bible and in Rabbinic literature established authoritative precedent for the performance of dream divination, contributing to its acceptance within Jewish culture, even if the practice never became part of the official cult.

Like dream techniques for causing or curing insomnia and for triggering nightmares or erotic dreams, practices for divining the future or acquiring knowledge of hidden things via dreams are based on the idea that dreaming can be managed, regulated and even provoked. These practices are part of a cultural strategy to know, experience and manipulate reality that was developed, enhanced and passed down by men and women. In Jewish culture, there are two main forms of dream divination. The first is dream interpretation, which organizes the content of dreams according to given cultural patterns to control and subdue the angst instigated by the inscrutability of dreams. The second is a technique known as dream request, through which a person induces revelatory dreams that are intelligible and meaningful for taking practical or spiritual choices in wakeful life.

One of the most widespread forms of divination practised in the premodern world, dream interpretation (oneiromancy) takes place in the *post-somnium* (i.e., the stage after dreaming). This concerns naturally occurring dreams, and usually requires the assistance of an expert. Dreamers recall and tell the content of their spontaneous dreams to a dream interpreter in the hope of gaining information about their future. Using different techniques, the interpreter analyses the dream content and associates each dream sign with a specific prognostic, thus providing a reading (i.e., an interpretation) to the dreamer. Part of the knowledge associated with oneiromancy is transmitted in oneirocritic manuals, anthologies of dreams that list dream signs (e.g., teeth falling out) and for each sign its related interpretation. Each entry in the list, consisting of a protasis (the dream sign) followed by an apodosis (its interpretation), takes the form 'if someone sees X, Y will follow'. While the most famous oneirocritic manual from the ancient world is the *Oneirocritica* by Artemidorus of Daldis (second century CE), excerpts from ancient Egyptian and Mesopotamian manuals of dream interpretation have been preserved as well.

The Hebrew Bible contains two remarkable Jewish paradigms of dream interpreters: Joseph and the prophet Daniel. However, it is late antique rabbinic literature that documents for the first time a developed theory of dreams, the existence of professional interpreters and the use of oneirocritic manuals in the Jewish world.

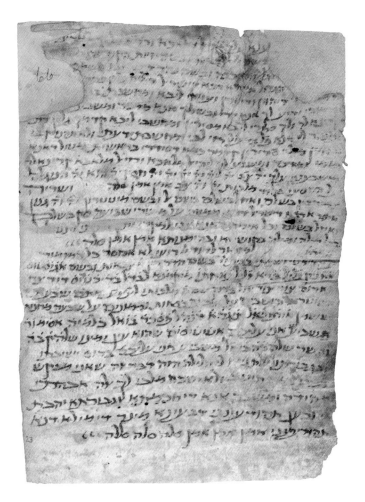

In particular, the Babylonian Talmud (*c.*500 CE) includes a long passage on dream interpretation, the so-called *Massekhet ha-Ḥalomot* or *Pereq ha-Ḥalomot* (*Tractate of Dreams* or *Chapter of Dreams*). Part of this can be regarded as an oneirocritic manual and it may once have circulated independently from its Talmudic context. As in non-Jewish oneirocritic manuals, the dream signs and

34 A recipe for *she'elat ḥalom* preserved on an eleventh- to twelfth-century fragment from the Cairo Genizah.

their corresponding interpretations are here organized into categories, such as dreams that relate to plants, animals, situations from daily life, people connected with Jewish religion, aspects of Jewish cult and biblical verses.

Manuals of dream interpretation also circulated among Jews during the medieval era, as demonstrated by many oneirocritic fragments found in the Cairo Genizah (i.e., the storeroom of the Ben Ezra Synagogue in Cairo where old documents could be safely discarded even if they were about sacred subjects), among which are copies in Judeo-Arabic of an oneirocritic manual attributed to Ḥai Gaon. However, the Jewish manual of oneiromancy that gained the most popularity was *Pitron Ḥalomot* by the rabbi and physician Solomon ben Jacob Almoli. The volume gathers material from both classical Jewish sources (such as biblical accounts on dreams, *Pereq ha-Ḥalomot*, Rashi, Maimonides and other famous halakhists and kabbalists) and non-Jewish sources (such as Plato, Aristotle, Averroes and Avicenna). It was published in Salonika *c.*1515–17 but also continued to circulate in manuscript form.

Related to dream interpretation is *hatavat ḥalom* (literally 'the melioration of a dream'), a technique for reversing a bad or unclear dream that causes distress in the dreamer. This practice – documented in the Babylonian Talmud (Berakhot 55b), as well as in later Jewish texts (e.g., in a few fragments from the Cairo Genizah, as well as in Almoli's treatise) – is used to avoid a negative prediction warned of by a dream. Like dream interpretation, the *hatavat ḥalom* is based on the firm conviction that it is the interpretation that makes the dream experience meaningful and potentially decisive in affecting real life. The Babylonian Talmud says that 'a dream that has not been interpreted is like a letter that has not been read' (Berakhot 56a). Thus, through the utterance of specific prayers and formulae, the impression of a troubling dream, which may contain a bad omen for the dreamer, is transformed into a sensation of peace.

A more domestic form of dream divination widespread in Jewish culture is the dream request, in Hebrew *she'elat ḥalom*. This is an activity that takes place mostly in the *ante-somnium* (i.e., the stage before dreaming). It concerns induced dreams and does not necessarily require the assistance of an expert. Through ritual sleep, the magical use of language and, to a lesser extent, the manipulation of elements, the *she'elat ḥalom* produces a dream, thus stimulating – rather than merely interpreting – the dream content.

The *she'elat ḥalom* was documented in Jewish sources from the tenth century onwards. Well rooted in earlier Jewish apocalyptic and divinatory traditions, it probably developed in late antiquity. Used by Jews from different socio-cultural backgrounds – men, women, rabbis, physicians, kabbalists (followers of the Jewish mystical tradition known as Kabbala), halakhists (experts in Jewish law) – it was performed to receive an answer to questions concerning day-to-day matters, such as the outcome of a commercial enterprise, the success of a spousal union, the prognosis of a sickness or the location of a lost inheritance, as well as to discover spiritual secrets or to clarify religious matters.

According to the sources, the ritual sleep – usually preceded by a three-day period during which ascetic norms were observed – was induced by the utterance of prayers and magical formulae. Sometimes, people would inscribe papers or parchments with details of a specific request and place them under the head when going to sleep. The content of the revelatory dream was expected in the form of specific dream signs to which a certain meaning was attributed in advance (e.g., biblical or Jewish figures or places for a good omen, non-Jewish figures or places for a bad omen), or as a direct encounter with a numinous being or a nonhuman entity who would verbally reveal the answer to the enquiry.

The fragments from the Cairo Genizah preserve several recipes and finished products (i.e., texts used in the divinatory technique itself) for *she'elat ḥalom*, one of which is shown in Fig. 34, which reproduces an eleventh- to twelfth-century fragment that originally belonged to a recipe book in the form of a *rotulus* (a long, thin scroll). This recipe combines different Jewish apocalyptic and magical traditions, instructing users to recite some of the Psalms, adjure the angels and recite a prayer for divination based on a passage from the book of Daniel. Recipes for *she'elat ḥalom* have also been transmitted in premodern codices of Jewish magic of European provenance. Easily accessible to everyone, the *she'elat ḥalom* has enjoyed remarkable popularity in Jewish culture and is sometimes practised even nowadays, as demonstrated by the instructions for engaging in this dream activity found on dedicated websites.

ASTROLOGY IN RENAISSANCE EUROPE

Michelle Aroney

In the Renaissance, astrology was a compulsory undergraduate subject at many universities throughout Europe. It was a highly skilled craft that relied on extensive mathematical and astronomical education. Astrology was highly valued because it could provide guidance on almost every aspect of life to clients from every level of society – from the poorest agricultural workers to the Holy Roman Emperor. Astrologers' consulting rooms were filled with people who sought advice on their relationships, travel plans, business ventures and, most extensively, their health.

Medicine and astrology were intimately linked in the premodern world. In late medieval and Renaissance Europe, it was not unusual for different varieties of medical practitioner to use astrological techniques in their everyday practice. Astrology was seen as a logical extension of medicine: both engaged in prognostication, and both saw the human body as a microcosm that was powerfully influenced by the macrocosm. Astrology was related to both the intellectual and practical sides of medicine, and became embedded in the medical curricula of European universities through a complex interplay between theory and practice.

Astrologers gave advice on all health concerns and at every point in a patient's healthcare journey. As they saw it, the movements of the heavenly bodies, in relation to each other and to the twelve signs of the zodiac, exert a powerful influence on earth. Planets produce injury and disease by impacting bodies directly and also by impacting the air. In the Galenic medicine of the Renaissance, health was believed to be determined by the balance of the four humours, black bile, yellow bile, phlegm and blood, which are themselves altered by planets imparting varying quantities of heat, cold, dryness and moisture.

The position of the celestial bodies in the heavens provided the physician with an understanding of propitious and inauspicious times to perform various therapeutic procedures, such as purges, fasting, bleeding and cautery, as well as the collection, compounding and administration of drugs. Each of the seven planets, twelve signs and twelve houses of the horoscope were linked to particular diseases and parts of the body. The so-called zodiac man, examples of which can be seen in Figs 6 and 35, illustrates how parts of the body were thought to be governed by different signs of the zodiac. There were warnings against performing a procedure when the moon was in the sign associated with that part of the body. In some European cities, medical and surgical guilds had regulations that called on practitioners to consult astrological almanacs before performing medical interventions.

Astrologers drew on these theories when prognosticating. Ptolemy had given the fourth and sixth houses governance over illness and death, and physicians could cast horoscopes for the exact moment when a disease began (or when the patient first consulted the practitioner) to access information about their health. An individual's predisposition to certain diseases was partly

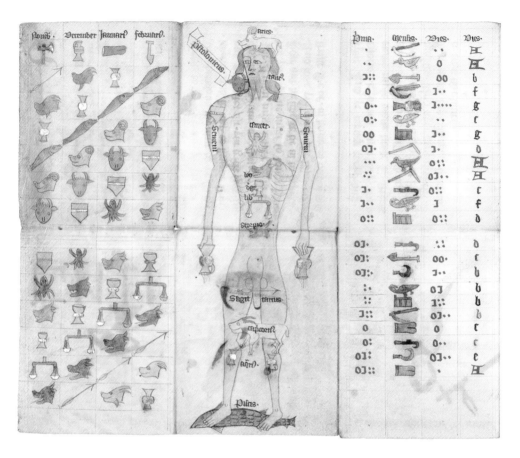

a product of the arrangement of the heavens at their birth and could therefore be analysed in light of their birth chart. The English astrologer Richard Napier made a successful business treating clients with astrology in this way. His surviving casebooks, a page of which can be seen in Fig. 13, shed light on the identity of his clients, who were from all levels of society, and the questions they asked, which covered just about the whole gamut of human experience in this period.

35 A zodiac man in a late fourteenth-century English collection of divinatory texts.

Astrologers were also interested in what we would today call public health. Here they used a technique called the horoscope for the revolution of the year. This horoscope mapped the heavens at the sun's annual entrance into the first degree of Aries, which happens every March at the spring equinox. The astrologer analysed the horoscope, taking into consideration the influence of the planet that was the lord of the year. It was also important to identify planetary conjunctions, especially Saturn–Jupiter conjunctions, which occur roughly every twenty years. Conjunctions herald momentous events on earth, including plague. Comets and eclipses could also be indicative of imminent epidemics.

The horoscope for the revolution of the year revealed the likelihood of population-level events such as famine, fire and flood and of the risk of endemic disease (e.g., madness, leprosy, ringworm) and epidemic disease (e.g., plague, smallpox). Astrologers published their findings in annual almanacs, which were some of the bestselling texts in Europe in this period. In a society where the assumptions underlying astrology were largely taken for granted, the value of such predictions was obvious. It is therefore no surprise that astrologers had long been crucial advisers in royal and princely courts throughout Europe and its colonies, as they were in the Ottoman Empire.

Astrologers were thus often successful in acquiring the patronage of leaders by dedicating their prognostications or theoretical or practical works to them; for example, the German astrologer and mathematician Petrus Apianus dedicated his *Astronomicum Caesareum* to the Holy Roman Emperor Charles V in 1540. This lavishly illustrated text – which was essentially a coffee-table

36 A dragon volvelle in Petrus Apianus's *Astronomicum Caesareum* (1540). Used in sequence with other volvelles in the book, this volvelle enabled eclipses to be calculated. In theories deriving from the Islamic world, the dragon's head (*caput draconis*) and tail (*cauda draconis*) represent the north and south lunar nodes and carry astrological significance.

LATITUDO LUNAE MERIDIONALIS

VMBRAERRE

LATITUDO LUNAE SEPTENTRION

CANCER ♋ GEMINI ♊ TAURUS ♉ ARIES ♈ PISCES ♓ AQUARIUS ♒ CAPRICORN ♑ SAGITTARIUS ♐ SCORPIUS ♏ LIBRA ♎ VIRGO ♍ LEO ♌

F III

book – included volvelles (one of which is pictured in fig. 36), that helped practitioners calculate the positions of the planets and celestial phenomena like eclipses.

Astrology could offer glory and prestige to both the practising physician and the discipline of medicine more generally. In a competitive medical marketplace, the learned physician stood out through not only his university education, but also his strong competence in astrology (universities did not admit women, and so university-educated astrologers were always male). There was a general sense that the excellence of astrology, which came from both its object (it studied the perfect heavens) and its effects (it allowed some degree of prediction), made those competent in the art superior to the uninitiated. Although predictions related to phenomena that seemed dependent on human free will were generally more suspect and were not approved by the Catholic Church, astrological prognostications relating to medicine, navigation and agriculture were much more widely accepted in the Renaissance. Astrological medicine remained widespread in Europe into the eighteenth century, especially among the broader public.

PALMISTRY IN BRITAIN AND THE UNITED STATES

Joan Navarre

> Could it be that written in his hand, in characters that he
> could not read himself, but that another could decipher,
> was some fearful secret of sin, some blood red sign
> of crime?
>
> Oscar Wilde, 'Lord Arthur Savile's Crime'[1]

During the waning years of the nineteenth century, an
enthusiasm for palmistry swept through Great Britain
and the United States of America. On both sides of the
Atlantic, people studied the lines in their hands to search
for clues about their future. Was wealth on the horizon?
Romance? A long life? The answer lay in the palm of
one's hand.

Palmistry, or cheiromancy, is an art that seeks insights
through consultation of the hand. Characters and
fortunes are told by inspection and interpretation of
both the shape of the hand and the lines on its palm.
Cheiromancy has a long history. Aristotle recognized the
important functions of the hand in his *History of Animals*,
which described how the lines of the hand could be used
to predict longevity. An ancient axiom informs all studies
of cheiromancy: 'know thyself'.

Cheiromancy continued to be practised in Christian
Europe into the medieval period. During the Renaissance,

however, it moved into the margins of social acceptance, seen as one of the seven forbidden arts, alongside necromancy; geomancy, the study of earth; aeromancy, the study of air; pyromancy, the study of fire; hydromancy, the study of water; and osteomancy, the study of bones (especially scapulars in scapulimancy). During the sixteenth century, cheiromancy was suppressed by the Catholic Church, with papal edicts issued against what were perceived to be dark arts.

In the nineteenth century, however, cheiromancy became more popular. In 1839 Captain Casimir Stanislas D'Arpentigny published *La chirognomie*, a work of cheiromancy based on his research into Renaissance practices. The book was later translated by a British polymath and Fellow of the Royal Society, Edward Heron-Allen. Heron-Allen almost single-handedly revived and systematized palmistry in the Victorian period, setting the stage for others to follow. In the nineteenth century, Rosa Baughan, Katherine St Hill and Cheiro (William John Warner) added their names to a growing roster of Victorians who studied, promoted and practised palmistry. The art was deeply popular among a wide variety of people. Cheiro, for example, enjoyed a colourful cast of clients, including the humorist Mark Twain, the French stage actor Sarah Bernhardt, President Grover Cleveland of the United States, the inventor Thomas Edison, the playwright Oscar Wilde and Edward, Prince of Wales.

During the 1880s, Heron-Allen published multiple books on palmistry, performed private séances and even lectured as a professor of palmistry in England and the United States. In several popular books, he celebrated palmistry as a science, presented a methodology for reading palms and addressed the duties and dangers of being a palm reader. To read and record the story of life and death

37 Cheiromantic drawings of both hands, with ornamental background, in a late medieval English compilation of medical manuscripts.

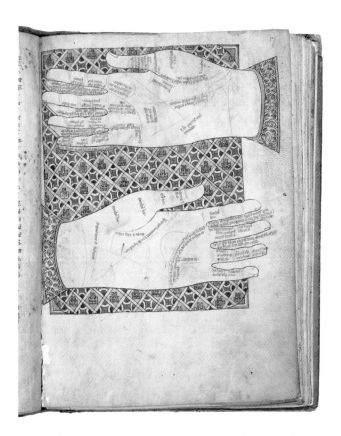

required patience and precision. For example, when the line of life, one of the main lines in the palm, is cut short, death's imminent arrival is declared. The palm reader must carefully inspect the appearance of this line and its proximity to other major lines, such as the line of head.

In light of the need for precision, Heron-Allen developed a specialized vocabulary. He popularized three technical terms, all starting with the Greek word *cheiro*, meaning 'hand': *cheiromancy* (as defined above), *cheirognomy* (divining by looking at the shape of the hand) and *cheirosophy* (hand wisdom or knowledge).

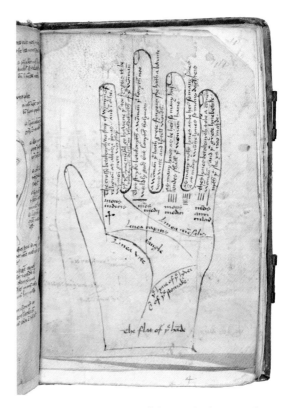

38 This sketch from fifteenth-century England describes the cheiromantic meaning of the lines of the palm and fingers. This hand describes prognostications for women, including, 'a woman that hath grete fyngers she hath a bownteous witte and lytell worth' and 'as many lynes as be her so many husbondes shall the woman have'.

Oscar Wilde was one of those who became fascinated with palmistry in the nineteenth century through the influence of Heron-Allen. In a letter of September 1886, Wilde addressed Heron-Allen as 'My dear Astrologer' and expressed great anticipation for the publication of his forthcoming book on palmistry that contained a pioneering classification system for hand shapes.

Over the course of their friendship, Heron-Allen studied Wilde's hand, diagrammed it and preserved the detailed sketch in an album filled with similar drawings of the palms of famous people. He exhibited and discussed his diagram of Wilde's hand while touring the United States as the darling of the public lecture circuit. The popular American periodical *The Daily Graphic* devoted a double-page spread on 17 November 1886 to 'Hand Reading' that contained an image of Wilde's hand and offered Heron-Allen's analysis:

> The hand of Oscar Wilde is also peculiar. It is very large and soft. The size indicates a great love of detail and a keen analytical power. The line of head, the first cross below the base of the fingers, is very strongly marked, showing extraordinary brain power and profound scholarship. In England there is hardly another so profound a scholar as Oscar Wilde. The small lines under the little finger evidence his great power of expression.

The palmistry revival of the late nineteenth century inspired societal innovations, literary creations and philosophical ruminations. Wilde's interest in palmistry, for example, surfaced in his literary writings. In 1887 Wilde published 'Lord Arthur Savile's Crime: A Story of Cheiromancy'. A parody of a murder mystery, the story is also a dark comedy about the importance of palm readers.

The setting is a London soirée, the characters are from fashionable society and the dominant theme addresses the duties and dangers of looking at the lines of the hand. The dialogue begins with Lady Windermere, a woman of the latest fashion who is devoted to palmistry, asking 'Where is my cheiromantist?' The characters reveal an understanding of the two main branches of the science of palmistry explained by Heron-Allen, *cheirognomy* and *cheiromancy*. As Lady Windermere states: 'He tells me I have a pure psychic hand, and that if my thumb had been the least bit shorter I would have been a confirmed pessimist, and gone into a convent.' She seems to understand the grammar of palmistry, as the psychic hand is one of the seven types presented in Heron-Allen's

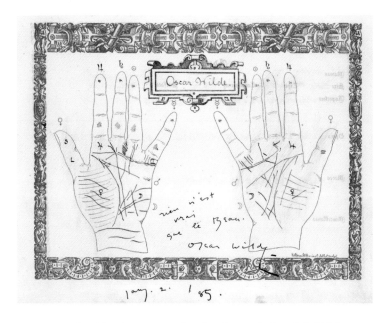

classification system for the shape of a hand. Wilde's comedy presents characters who use and occasionally question Heron-Allen's key terms, his scientific approach to palmistry and his theme of duty ('know thyself').[2]

By the end of the nineteenth century, palmistry's popularity had faded in both England and the United States, and palm readers were no longer in the limelight. Instead, authorities called on the iron fist of the law – section 4 of the Vagrancy Act 1824, 'Persons committing certain Offences to be deemed Rogues and Vagabonds', including 'every Person pretending or professing to tell Fortunes, or using any subtle Craft, Means, or Device, by Palmistry or otherwise, to deceive and impose on any of His Majesty's Subjects'.[3] Subjected to religious, political and social prejudice and deemed a threat to the social order, the ancient practice of palmistry retreated to the margins of society even if it never completely went away.

39 Oscar Wilde's hands (as sketched by Heron-Allen), with Wilde's signature and the phrase 'Rien n'est vrai que le Beau' ('nothing is true but Beauty').

DIVINATION
IN CHINA

William Matthews

The earliest written records from China are records of divination. These are the famous oracle bones, the shoulder blades of oxen and lower shells of turtles, used by the Shang kings (*c.*1200–1050 BCE) to ask their ancestors and the high god Di about crucial affairs of state. We know little about the ceremony, but the divination was performed by applying a heated metal rod to the bone or shell. This would cause it to crack, and the pattern of cracking was read as indicating what would happen.

However, with the evolution of cosmology and political rule in the centuries following the Shang, up to the unification of China in 221 BCE, divination developed into something very different. The high god Di was replaced by a concept of heaven (*tian*), at first a personal god but later an impersonal force acting on the cosmos in dynamic relation to earth (*di*) and humanity (*ren*).

This came together with the development of an important idea, that knowledge of the underlying principles of the cosmos could be gained through observation of the natural world. This is presented explicitly in the commentaries of the *Yijing*, or *I Ching* (*Book of Changes*), a divination manual consisting of sixty-four hexagrams, six-line diagrams understood as indices of cosmic conditions, that has had an enormous influence on Chinese culture. Such principles were, and continue to be, used to identify the propensities of heaven and to understand cosmic cycles of change.

By the time of China's second imperial dynasty, the Han (206 BCE–220 CE), this cosmology had become highly systematized. The cosmos was understood to be composed of a single energy substance, *qi,* which is continuously transforming through five phases (*wuxing*) that interact with each other in constructive or destructive ways based on the principles of *yin* and *yang,* yielding and advancing. This framework, often called *correlative cosmology* in the academic literature, formed a basis for dynastic legitimacy, with dynasties rising and falling according to the cycle of *qi*. It also formed the basis for a huge range of divination techniques, and continues to do so today, along with other disciplines including martial arts and Chinese medicine.

Today, the most widespread forms of divination that rely on this cosmology are *feng shui* (a type of geomancy), *bazi* (horoscopy) and *Yijing* fate calculation. These are used for distinct purposes, and often in conjunction with each other. All rely on correlative cosmology, in which all phenomena in the cosmos, including objects, time, directions and emotions, can be classified according to the five phases of *qi*.

Feng shui is concerned with maximising the flows of auspicious *qi* in one's immediate environment. This is typically done using a compass (*luopan*) detailed with key cosmological correlates, which are used to determine the effects of *qi* flows in different directions. In rural areas this is often used to determine a sound location for the siting of a new house; in urban contexts, prospective residents may consult a *feng shui* specialist to determine the auspiciousness of a prospective new home.

40 Pyromancy is the divinatory practice whereby bones, usually from an ox or turtle, are used to answer difficult questions. Questions were carved into the object, which was heated until the bone cracked. The cracks formed patterns that could be interpreted. This oracle bone dates from the Shang Dynasty in China, c.1200–1050 BCE.

Feng shui readily combines with *bazi*. This sort of horoscopy is based on a calendrical system, in contrast to astrology's concern with the movement and position of celestial bodies. (There is a Chinese form of astrology, following the *ziwei doushu* method (purple star astrology) that can also be combined with *bazi*.) The most common form of horoscopy in China today is based on a person's eight characters (*bazi*), which refer to the year, month, day and time of birth according to a calendar based on sixty-year cycles of ten Heavenly Stems and twelve Earthly Branches, the ultimate origins of which can be traced back to the Shang dynasty. Each stem and branch correlates with a phase of *qi*, and the year, month, day and time are respectively identified by a combination of a stem and a branch. This allows a diviner to identify the *qi* governing a person's birth, and to use this to extrapolate their fate across their lifespan in ten-year periods, based on how their *qi* interacts with that of different years. People will typically go for *bazi* consultations at the lunar new year, to obtain a forecast for the year ahead or to assess their compatibility with a partner. When it is combined with *feng shui*, *bazi* offers a means of assessing the compatibility of a person with a place; on this basis, certain homes will be more or less suitable for different people.

Correlative cosmology also underpins various divination techniques based on the *Yijing*. Traditionally, this was done by manipulating dried yarrow stalks, but today the most common method uses coins to derive one of the text's sixty-four hexagrams. Each of these lines is correlated with one of the

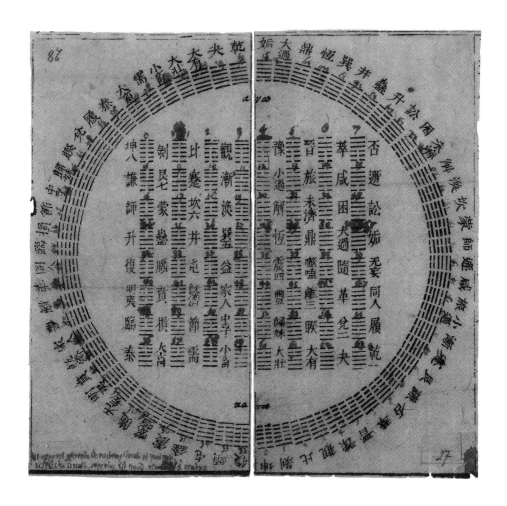

41 Diagram of the *Yijing* belonging to the German mathematician and philosopher Gottfried Wilhelm Leibniz, who annotated it with Roman numerals.

five phases, and can thus be used in a similar way to correlates in *feng shui* and horoscopy – and is likewise compatible with these. While horoscopy is used to understand fate over one's life course, *Yijing* divination is used to enquire about more immediate concerns. These might be major life events, such as getting married, moving home, embarking on a new career or securing a business deal. The method is popular because, through its use of a systematic cosmology, it reduces the uncertainty inherent in such decisions in a way that is essentially morally neutral.

In addition to the popularity of these techniques across Chinese society, divination involving gods and ancestors continues to exist and is often used in conjunction with them. In temples across China, people approach local gods and deities from the Daoist and Buddhist pantheons to seek information about what will happen. This is commonly done by dropping pairs of small wooden blocks and examining how they fall or by casting lots. The other main means by which gods are consulted is through spirit mediums who, it is believed, can become possessed by a specific god. This practice is especially prevalent in Chinese diaspora communities across South-East Asia.

The government of the People's Republic of China generally considers divination to be superstition and carries out periodic crackdowns. However, divination has continued to be hugely popular as the country rapidly modernized over the past four decades, creating an environment of risk and opportunity. As well as perennial concerns with marriage compatibility, queries commonly concern promotion prospects, when and where to move house, the likely success of business deals, and – as has recently been reported as a driver of increased temple visits among the growing unemployed youth – exam results and employment possibilities. Despite the political and social promotion of science and modernization, there are some problems they cannot answer. In such a context, divination provides an aid to decision-making and a means of reducing uncertainty.

42 A Chinese diviner from a nineteenth-century album of paintings depicting various skilled trades.

TIBETAN ROPE DIVINATION

Alexander K. Smith

There are many different forms of divination practised across the Tibetan-speaking world. These range from the cryptic and sometimes spectacular performances of oracles to the precise mathematical calculations of astrologers, many of whom practise in monasteries. Divination is also commonly done with certain household objects, including rice, salt, stones, dice, knotted ropes, rosaries and mirrors, as well as through the burning of sheep scapulae. These methods are used to answer a wide variety of questions, from everyday problems (such as misplaced items, theft and medical issues) to questions of profound spiritual importance, even going so far as to address an individual's karma, potential demonic influence and death.

In Tibetan Buddhist cultures, human beings are believed to be subject to various natural and supernatural powers, including the planets and stars, countless demons, demi-gods and regional spirits. Divination practices provide a window through which clients are able to see and understand the elemental and supernatural forces that affect their lives, allowing them to take appropriate action to potentially change their future. Therefore divination provides an indispensable tool for everyday living and, despite the pressures of the modern diaspora, is still widely consulted.

Ju thig (pronounced joo-tig), a particular form of Tibetan rope divination, is an excellent example of how many basic forms of divination are practised across the Tibetan cultural sphere. To perform at least a minimal form of *ju thig*, the diviner requires an appropriate divination text and six ropes: five lesser cords measuring roughly three feet in length; and a longer sixth cord known as the divination guide, which measures roughly six feet. As the diviner ties nooses and knots into the ends of each rope, they typically recite a series of invocations, inviting specific deities to oversee the casting to increase the divination's accuracy. Once this is complete, the ropes are bundled together and cast vigorously to the ground. The diviner then refers to an appropriate divination manual to interpret the patterns formed by the casting, focusing on the location and shape of the nooses in relation to the cardinal and intercardinal directions. The diviner's job, then, is to translate and contextualize the text's often cryptic passages so as to provide the client with a satisfactory answer to their question.

opposite

43 Tibetan rope divination in action. Here *ju thig* cords are being cast to the ground, with pebble divination mat and pebbles prominently displayed.

below

44 A cross-section of a nineteenth-century rope divination manual featuring illustrations of configurations of ropes and nooses and their associated prognostications.

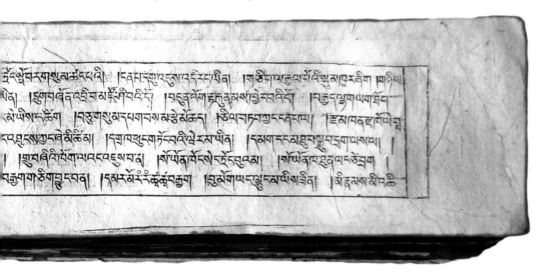

As with many other forms of Tibetan divination, the clients who seek out ritual specialists and request *ju thig* castings can come from any walk of life. On a busy day, a diviner's waiting room has the feel of a village doctor's office. Rich and poor rub shoulders and clients, monastic and lay, often sit quietly, reflecting on their questions or sharing small talk with strangers. The diviner's clients also often pay the diviner a small amount of money for their divination or in kind with offerings of various goods, including barley flour, coffee and tea, and make a donation to a monastery or charity at the diviner's behest.

But who are the Tibetan diviners themselves? Following an illness or traumatic event, some of them act as oracles, having learned to develop and cultivate the capacity for spirit possession. However, being a diviner is not bound to a single profession, sex or method. For example, some diviners learn the art of divination out of an interest in esoteric ritual practices or as part of a mentorship with an accomplished ritual specialist, while others begin to perform divination for purely practical or financial reasons. There are very few rules or regulations stipulating who can and cannot perform simple castings, although divinations performed by educated monks and/or respected spiritual adepts are more highly prized than those performed by lay people in their home environments.

45 An eighteenth-century depiction of Buddha sTon pa gShen rab teaching divination. The figure in the centre of the panel, dressed in red and sitting cross-legged in front of a white mat, is holding *ju thig* divination cords.

Particularly skilled diviners also often supplement their income through client consultations, and it is not uncommon to meet specialists in divination who have mastered multiple techniques that they use, as appropriate, for different clients in different social settings. In that sense, diviners can serve many different roles in their communities, providing, for example,

resources for conflict resolution, medical consultations and religious guidance as well as practical worldly advice.

Where did Tibetan divination practices come from? Tibetan divination as it exists today is extremely eclectic and appears to be a mixture of Indian, Chinese, Turkic and Indigenous Tibetan elements. In some instances, the cultural and historical origins of a particular tradition are relatively clear: for example, a great deal of Tibetan astrology clearly shows Chinese and Indian influences. The origins of other practices, however, are much more difficult to articulate. Early Tibetan rope divination texts combine Turkic, Central Asian and Indigenous Tibetan concepts. As a consequence, modern scholars have largely abandoned efforts to find a single 'pure' origin for Tibetan divination, and instead view Tibetan divination practices as a complex and unique amalgam of South, Central and East Asian ritual traditions.

NUOSU EGG DIVINATION

Katherine Swancutt

In the Liangshan (Cool Mountains) of Southwest China, egg divination is popular among the Nuosu, a Tibeto-Burman group also known by their Chinese ethnonym of Yi. Many Nuosu people divine using a variety of items, and in particular chicken thigh and tongue bones. But Nuosu priests (*bimo* ᚠ ᚡ), male shamans (*sunyi* ᚢᚣ) and female shamans (*monyi* ᚤᚥ) often divine by cracking a raw egg into a traditional wooden lacquerware bowl. The bowls are painted black inside and are half-filled with water, so that when a raw egg is poured into them, the bubbles it produces can be clearly seen.

Before cracking open an egg, diviners ask what illnesses and other troubles their clients are facing. Many clients seek help for skin problems, rheumatic joints, persistent headaches, dizziness, pain in an arm or other limb, and other physical ailments. Illnesses like these are often attributed to the spirits of specific diseases, to disgruntled spirits of the landscape and even to the wily ghosts of the Nuosu and people of other ethnic backgrounds. Usually, Nuosu people become ill or face other problems after they encounter ghosts and spirits in their living environments, including their households and livestock pens, the roads around their homes, and nearby mountains.

To find out which spirits or ghosts are responsible, diviners summon their spirit helpers and the guardian spirits of their client's household to help them perform an egg divination. They may rub artemisia over the egg to purify it before gently striking its side with the blunt edge of a knife to produce hairline cracks in its shell. As shown in Fig. 46, diviners then hand the egg to their clients, who often hold it to their lips and blow into it so that the egg will 'inhale' their bodily illnesses, especially through these cracks. Clients usually also rub the egg across their arms, legs, shoulders and torso so that the egg further inhales their illnesses. The egg is then ready to reveal which of the many possible ghosts or spirits could be the source of the problem.

After retrieving the egg from their client, diviners crack it into a lacquerware bowl and use a knife or the empty eggshell halves to score its yolk into quarters. Opening up the yolk is analogous to opening up the client's body. Both the egg and its yolk typically represent the client, while the water in the bowl frequently represents the client's living environment. Once the yolk has been scored open, diviners may use half of an empty eggshell to scoop up some water from the bowl and pour it back again, which generates bubbles in the bowl. Bubbles may be pinhead-sized, more substantial or grouped together in clusters. Most bubbles tend to appear on the surface of the water, but some are trapped beneath it. Some bubbles stand out because they are close to or some distance away from the egg yolk. Each detail matters because the bubbles are interpreted according to their size, their proximity to the yolk, whether they appear in a cluster of bubbles or alone and whether they lie on the water's surface or are submerged.

Diviners may take one look at the bubbles and know, or at least have a hunch about, the ghosts or spirits that

are present and the illnesses or problems they may have caused. Pointing at specific bubbles with the knife used to crack open the egg, or with just a twig picked up from the ground, diviners explain to their clients which ghosts or spirits the bubbles represent and why. Clients may also use a twig to point at bubbles, asking if they represent the ghosts that they suspect have been haunting them for some time. A Nuosu person may, for example, ask whether the ghosts of forlorn relatives who lack descendants have entered their living environments in search of food, drink and the warmth of the household hearth. But, while bubbles are meant to represent specific ghosts and spirits, Nuosu people tend to speak carefully during divinations. Caution is needed because wily

46 At the start of egg divination, a Nuosu client blows into an egg, which 'inhales' his illlness.

ghosts and spirits are never far away from the client who is being haunted, and may strike again at any moment.

Sometimes the diviner may sense that more ghosts and spirits are afoot than they had expected. When this happens, they often scoop up and pour more water onto the egg to create further bubbles. These fresh bubbles may reveal the presence of additional ghosts or spirits. Examining the bubbles again, diviners double-check the source of their client's troubles and identify any other troublesome ghosts or spirits that they find. Since ghosts and spirits are crafty, diviners need to be crafty and creative too. They act like sleuths who reveal the many ghosts and spirits that try to evade detection. The creative and even spontaneous hunches, thoughts and actions of diviners therefore lie at the heart of egg divination.

47 Here the diviner points a stick at a bubble to reveal the ghost or spirit responsible for the client's illnesses during an egg divination.

Each diviner focuses on the same kinds of bubbles but may interpret them somewhat differently. A particular diviner may even interpret the same kinds of bubbles differently from one divination to the next.

When an egg divination is complete, the diviner collects the eggshells, any twigs used to point at bubbles and any sprigs of artemisia used for purifying the egg. These items are placed into the lacquerware bowl and may be waved in a circular motion while the diviner sends the spirit helpers and guardian spirits back to their usual places. Because everything in the human world is inverted in the spirit world, which diviners and clients aim to please, the usual circular direction is often inverted so that the bowl is waved clockwise over female clients and anticlockwise over male clients. The contents of the bowl are then poured out in a location that will not attract any unwanted ghosts or spirits back to the client's living environment.

48 A Nuosu priest pours water from the lacquerware bowl back onto the egg while divining.

P. 52

Coup de 27

Ce talon du jeu tombe au néant
et s'explicque ainsi.

CARTOMANCY IN EUROPE

Emily E. Augur

Playing cards as they are known in Europe and North America today were invented sometime after the development of paper, which originated in China in 105 CE. Paper proved so well suited to drawing and writing that it replaced both papyrus and parchment. European paper mills were built in Spain from the late eleventh century, in Italy, France and Holland in the 1340s, and elsewhere in the decades and centuries that followed. Documents referring to playing cards made from paper appear in Europe from the 1360s and include both purchase orders and prohibitions on their use in gambling, which was considered a sin and a threat to moral and financial stability, and on their importation because they were a threat to local businesses and tax collectors.

It is entirely possible that the use of playing cards for fortune telling in Europe followed very closely on their arrival. If they were so used by women, particularly peasant women, the practice may well have escaped the written record for some time. Israhel van Meckenem's print, known as 'The Fortune Teller' (1490s), may be the earliest visual evidence of cartomancy, but the exact subject matter of this and later representations of playing card use continues to be debated. By the fifteenth century,

49 The French occultist Etteilla taught cartomancy methods in his books. In this spread he lays out a thirty-two-card piquet deck with an added etteilla card to represent the querent (identified here with the number one). Three rows of nine cards are read in different combinations according to the associations with people, qualities, actions and so on, that Etteilla provided, while the six cards at the bottom represent things the querent is to leave behind (Jean-Baptiste Alliette, *Etteilla, ou, Maniere de se recreer avec un jeu de cartes*, 1770).

allegorical interpretations, which varied from country to country, were certainly being applied to the suits, and documents setting out the cards' different associations became increasingly common in the years that followed. The earliest printed work to describe the use of playing cards for fortune telling, a kind of sortilege, was published in Venice in 1540. *Le sorti di Francesco Marcolino da Forli* (*The Oracles of Francesco Marcolini da Forli*) asks the user to draw one or two cards and then to refer to answers associated with those cards in the book. The method was evidently modelled on another volume printed in 1526, also in Venice, that focused on astrology and asked the consultant to roll dice or spin a dial to determine which lines in the volume would answer the query.

There are many indications that the images on the cards, even in gaming contexts, sometimes gave rise to imaginative associations with particular individuals and their destinies, but it is not until the seventeenth century that there is definite evidence of fortunes being read by laying out and reading the cards themselves in the transcripts of Spanish witchcraft trials and in European and English plays, stories, and visual art. As fortune telling with cards gained enough popularity to outweigh its notoriety, it is no surprise that enterprising publishers realized they could profit by printing decks with the divinatory meanings directly on the cards, thereby eliminating the need for extensive memorization or book consultation.

Most famously, Jean-Baptiste Alliette, better known by the reversed spelling of his surname as Etteilla, coined the term *cartonomancy*, which soon became cartomancy, for divination with cards. He also published a book on the subject in 1770 that provided meanings for the thirty-two cards of the piquet deck, including the court cards of king,

50 In this striking portrait, the British painter Wyndham Lewis depicts his wife as a cartomancer. The painting is entitled *La Suerte*, the Spanish for 'fate' or 'fortune' (oil on canvas, 1938).

queen and jack; the suits of hearts, diamonds, clubs, and spades; the aces; and the pips from seven to ten. An extra card called *etteilla* was included in his deck to represent the questioner.

Etteilla's popularity helped to professionalize cartomancy. By his own account, 150 of his roughly 500 students became professional practitioners. His work paved the way for the likes of Mademoiselle Le Normand, who became the most famous of many early nineteenth-century Parisian card readers and whose name is still associated with at least two different fortune-telling decks. In addition, Etteilla's books and ideas were a pivotal inspiration for the Hermetic Order of the Golden Dawn, founded in London in 1888.

The use of cards for divination by members of the Golden Dawn was also influenced by the so-called classic English method of card cutting. It involved selecting a significator and laying out the entire deck of fifty-two cards in five rows of nine and a sixth row of seven. This method has continued to be used up to the present day, with some changes to the card interpretations through the nineteenth century.

Early writers on cartomancy tended to assume that querents were all women and should be represented or signified by one of the queens, although some allow for both genders and the use of any queen or king. In 1920 Charles Platt narrowed the choice of significator by associating suits with complexion types, possibly taking his cue from directions laid out for tarot a decade earlier. This significator, however it is chosen, is always number one, and every ninth card from it is interpreted, with clubs indicating happiness, hearts joy and good temper, diamonds delays and quarrels, and spades serious problems, such as grief, sickness and death.

51 These fortune-telling cards were collected by the merchant and lawyer Francis Douce. To use them, one picks from a list of questions on the kings cards (e.g., 'Whether they shall return') before following a complex path through the sphere, queen and knave cards until an answer is found (e.g., 'They'd rather burn, than return').

Breslaw's Last Legacy; or, The Magical Companion (1784) proposed a unique response to the ever popular question 'Will my wish come true?' Here the querent randomly chooses a card to represent the wish, shuffles all the cards and cuts them into three piles. If the wish card is found next to the significator or the ace of hearts, the wish will be granted, but if the nine of spades is beside it the opposite will happen. The question may be asked three times to confirm the answer. Later authors repeat these instructions. Others, however, add the nine of hearts to the positive indicators, and allow for the mere presence of any of the three positives in the same pile with the wish card as offering hope for the desired outcome in the distant future. Thus, while there is obvious continuity in the cartomancy methods laid out in these texts, there is also variability over time. That variability was, and still is, undoubtedly greater in cartomancy traditions passed on orally.

BURYAT MONGOLIAN CARD DIVINATION

Katherine Swancutt

Diviners across Mongolia make use of various implements in their divinatory practices. These might include stones or coins, a strand of rosary beads, sheep scapulae that are burnt, sheep knucklebones that are tossed or a six-sided dice that is cast. With the help of their ancestors, shamanic spirits or Buddhist gods, Mongolian diviners may interpret these items to answer a variety of questions.

Buryat Mongols are ethnic minorities in the northeast of Mongolia, China and Russia, who often divine with playing cards. Many Buryat diviners are shamans, who are called *böö* if they are men and *udgan* if they are women. Shamans with the highest recognized powers are called *zaarin*. Some Buryats are even self-styled lama-shamans called *lam-böö*, who practise as both Buddhist lamas and shamans. Buryats use many kinds of card divination, but their most usual method is called Twenty Card. Twenty Card uses just the aces, kings, queens, jacks and tens from an ordinary playing card deck. Drawing on the assistance of their spirits, diviners use these cards to answer all sorts of questions, such as 'Will I receive a good score on my exam if I obtain a blessing from the spirits?', 'When will the car that I have commissioned to be driven from Russia to Mongolia arrive so that I can

sell it to a rich person?' or 'Was it my good friend, the nearby shaman, who cursed me?'

Twenty Card requires that the cards first be shuffled by a diviner. They may cut the deck using a special process to ensure that the first card used will not be associated with low fortune or stop the divination too soon. To do this, the diviner holds the cards face down in one hand, and then raises a portion of the deck away from the rest so that it is possible to identify just one card within it. This act is repeated until an auspicious card is found, which is moved to the bottom of the deck so that the divining process can begin. Usually, the diviner deals the cards face up or face down into an arrangement of five columns by four rows, although it is also possible to divine using four rows by five columns.

One reason for the popularity of Twenty Card is probably that it offers a ready-made template of the world writ small. Fig. 53 shows that the cards are – just as in a game of solitaire – always envisioned in relation to their optimal layout. Read from left to right, the optimal layout

starts with a column of aces that are associated with the home, followed by a column of kings (associated with men), a column of queens (associated with women), a column of jacks (associated with brothers or friends) and a column of tens (associated with the road). Typically, the kings, queens and jacks all represent actual people known to the clients and possibly also the diviners, with the red suits evoking people with a light complexion and the black suits evoking people with a dark complexion. From top to bottom, the rows move progressively from the suit of hearts (associated with joy) to diamonds (associated with success), to clubs (associated with speech) and to spades (associated with an obstacle or something hidden or shut off). Hearts are generally preferred to diamonds, just as clubs are preferred to spades.

After dealing the cards, the diviner begins to swap them around so that they reach the optimal layout or get as close to it as possible. The diviner first picks up the card in the lower right-hand corner and, placing it into its optimal position, picks up the card that happens to be

52 The Mongolian *Manual of Astrology and Divination* has helped determine auspicious times for particular activities, such as embarking on a new travel or business venture. This page, copied sometime in the nineteenth century, contains charts used to calculate the positions of Saturn (far left), which was relevant for the health of the knees and legs, and of solar eclipses (far right).

there already. Then the diviner swaps this new card with whatever card has happened to land in its own optimal position. This swapping process continues until the ten of spades lands in the lower right-hand corner. Since the ten of spades is always the last card placed, no cards can be swapped once it lands in its optimal position, which is why some diviners cut the deck to ensure that they do not start with this somewhat inauspicious card, which would stop a divination too soon. Sometimes all twenty cards reach their optimal layout through the swapping process, indicating that the best possible result has been reached. However, when everyone knows a serious problem is afoot, the optimal layout may be interpreted as a sampling error or even as a sarcastic response from the diviner's spirits, who are using it to show that the wrong answer was given because the wrong question was asked!

Any cards that end up out of their position in the optimal layout tend to stand out to diviners and clients, who may discuss, debate and closely examine them. Some clients may even push to interpret the cards in a specific way, but diviners have the final say on this. Cards that land in their optimal positions are usually ignored and allowed to fade into the background. Buryats are often keen to see what people (kings, queens or jacks) land in the home or road columns. The road refers not just to the paths that people travel but also to the wider world outside the home. Business partners might appear in the home column, indicating that money will come to the household. Relatives might appear in the road column, showing that they are on their way. Shamans or their spirit helpers may appear in the home column, suggesting that their curses have harmed someone in the household.

Numerous interpretations may arise, prompting Buryats to request follow-up divinations that sometimes

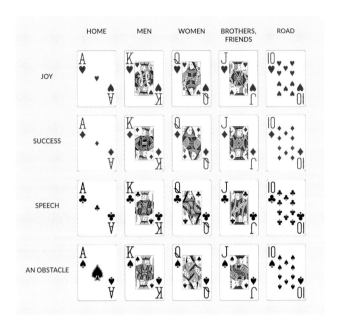

	HOME	MEN	WOMEN	BROTHERS, FRIENDS	ROAD
JOY	A♥	K♥	Q♥	J♥	10♥
SUCCESS	A♦	K♦	Q♦	J♦	10♦
SPEECH	A♣	K♣	Q♣	J♣	10♣
AN OBSTACLE	A♠	K♠	Q♠	J♠	10♠

go on for hours. Everything goes well when the diviner controls the cards so that they only represent what people are divining about and do not become more than representations. Occasionally, though, the diviner fails to control the cards. When this happens, the spirit helpers of rival shamans may hijack a particular card, imbue it with their presence and use it as a springboard to harm anyone present at the divination. They may even cause the diviner, the clients or both to lose their *süns*, which is like a soul or a kind of vital force that may leave the person's body. Since diviners cannot divine without their *süns* – and any person who loses their *süns* becomes ill – rituals need to be held to call them back. Fortunately, the cards are usually well controlled, and Buryats turn to their favourite diviners and to Twenty Card time and again whenever an important question arises.

53 The optimal layout for Twenty Card, a Buryat Mongolian form of divination.

อนึ่งพระยาภิมสาน เมื่อไปกินเมือง แทงกองทีป ผนวง
จ่มิขึ ยังก่าขุเม เปรชีเเล เหนกงวยยังมก
ช๊อปไจย ท๊องโคคิๅกสัง ภาท่านๅๅๅานๅๅรๅามๅภา
ๅๅกๅามๅๅช่นะ ภาไปยๅๅใคสๅบ ภาใๅๅๅาๅไๅยทๅๅย
ภาๅๅๅๅๅ หๅๅยๅๅมๅๅๅ

KHMER DIVINATION

Napakadol Kittisenee

Cambodian society embraces various prophetic traditions, including the Indian Vedic, Chinese/ Daoist astrological, Buddhist prophetic and various Indigenous animist methods of revealing the past, present and future. Within this Buddhist-inflected tradition, a person's life is not predetermined by divine interventions but by the results of their own actions (including in previous lives) or *karma* (*kamm* in Khmer). The way the present and future situations unfold thereby follows the shadow of an individual's past. Nevertheless, not every Khmer has a clear knowledge and vision of how their own past factors into their current and future conditions. In a society whose history is laced with violence and displacement, the past is often lost, the present fraught and the future uncertain. In these conditions, Khmer people regularly seek advice from diviners.

A *grū dāy* (from Sanskrit *guru* and a Khmer term meaning 'to predict') is a diviner who can read others' past, present and future. A *grū dāy* might be a Buddhist monk, a layperson (*acār*) or a spirit medium (*gru bāramī*). In various cases, a *grū dāy* may make use of a *damnāy* text (a prophecy manuscript) to help them. Some *grū dāy* may read fortunes using their client's

54 A page from *Tamra Sastra*, a nineteenth-century southern Thai fortune-telling manuscript used for *Kān Thǣng Sāttrā*, which is similar to a method of Khmer divination.

141

palms, face and/or birth date and time, through conversation or by using physical contact. *Grū dāy* of this kind possess special skills, such as the ability to read people's intentions or the future, and intuition. This spiritual power is widely accepted in many parts of the Buddhist world. A person can be born with this ability but they can also obtain it through long and intense meditation training.

The other kind of *grū dāy*, called *grū bāramī*, are spirit mediums. They earn their *riddhi* (higher powers for predictive visions) by using their body to channel powers from potent deities and spirits. Most *grū dāy* not only reveal future events but also offer guidance for preventing negative predictions from becoming reality.

Cák gambhīr is the most popular prophetic cultural practice in Cambodia. A combination of the Khmer term *cák* (to pierce/inject) and the Sanskrit term *gambhīr* (mantra, canon, text, treatise, manuscript), *cák gambhīr* refers to using a pointed or sharp wooden stick to make holes in a small folding palm-leaf manuscript (*sāstrā sleuk rith*) to pick pages. Each page of the sacred booklets used for this contains episodes from *Jātaka*, the Buddha's previous lives. In this context, the biographies of the Buddha serve as a mirror image of human life or a guiding prophecy for the client's life circumstances.

In practice, the client takes up the *gambhīr* and prays before the Buddha image or a statue of their revered spirit, asking that their powers will facilitate an accurate prediction. The client then places this small manuscript on top of their head and uses the stick to pick a random page. Most often, the interpretation of this chosen page from the predictive text is assisted by an *acār*, a layperson or ritual expert who usually serves as the caretaker of the sacred shrine or Buddhist monastery. The *acār* will help translate what the message means for the devotee's life. A similar practice called *Kān Thǣng Sāttrā* can also be found in southern Thailand.

The most important factor in obtaining an accurate prediction is where the ritual occurs. The best sites for performing the ritual are Deb Pranam, a Buddha statue in Angkor Thom; Braḥ Ang Cek Braḥ Ang Cam, a shrine in Siem Reap; Prāsāt Nagar Bājăy in Kampong Cham; and the pavilion of Braḥ Go in the Royal Palace in Phnom Penh.

Before making important plans, most Khmer people also consult a manual called *Siavbhau Mahā Sangkrānt* (*Khmer New Year Booklet*). Besides listing national holidays and Buddhist occasions, the book also specifies auspicious and inauspicious days. Auspicious days are those on which it is appropriate to hold important events such as weddings, to open a new building, to begin construction of a temple or to celebrate a new house. *Siavbhau Mahā Sangkrānt* is updated every year and is available for sale at marketplaces and bookshops in advance of the Khmer New Year in mid-April. Currently the most popular *Siavbhau Mahā Sangkrānt* is made by a renowned Sino-Khmer astrologer. Many people use this booklet, a hybrid text informed by both Gregorian and zodiac lunar calendrical systems, as their regular calendar.

Divination is also used at a societal level in Cambodia. *Buddh Damnāy* (Buddha's Prophecy) and *Ind Damnāy* (Indra Prophecy) both play a vital role in the Khmer people's perception of their own history. Based on a strong oral tradition, these prophecies are also common in Theravāda Buddhist countries such as Sri Lanka, Thailand, Burma and Laos. Their exact origins are unclear, but the texts claim to be composed at the apogee of the Khmer Empire during the last millennium. Although they were written during a golden age, these texts predict a catastrophic future. The apocalyptic texts *Buddh Damnāy* and *Ind Damnāy* predict great atrocities and social upheaval, and urge people not to be careless and to cultivate good karma. Yet, after this societal and moral decline, they predict that Cambodia will rise again with the assistance of a virtuous messianic leader.

These texts overlap with some of the Theravāda Buddhist commentaries that circulate in the region, but with the addition of local interpretations on how the crisis is made manifest in society and how society can be regenerated. After the Cambodian genocide (1975–79), particularly in the 1980s and early 1990s, Khmer people realized that the prophecy had in many ways been actualized in the traumatic events they had experienced, and some look for the predicted virtuous leader to help save the war-torn country.

Divination continues to thrive in Khmer society today. People seek prophetic advice through various means and disparate local sources to navigate uncertainties and precarious conditions. Divination functions like a map to guide their journey through life.

ZANDE DIVINATION

Margaret Buckner

The Zande (or Azande, using the Zande plural prefix *a*-) live along the Nile–Congo watershed where the three modern-day countries of the Democratic Republic of the Congo, South Sudan and Central African Republic meet. Popular in anthropological literature thanks to the works of the British anthropologist E.E. Evans-Pritchard, the Zande are known for their political organization (kingdoms), their Trickster tales, their harp music and perhaps especially their beliefs in witchcraft, magic and oracles.

The Zande believe that illness, death and other misfortunes are due to the ill will of a fellow human rather than to coincidence or bad luck. For the Zande, two types of causes combine to cause misfortune. The sensitive cause, often visible, is accessible to the senses on the level of common sense, while the mystical cause is invisible and explains why a particular person suffered a particular misfortune in a particular place at a particular time. To use Evans-Pritchard's classic example, if a granary collapses, killing the people resting beneath it, the sensitive cause would be the termites that have obviously eaten through the wooden posts, but only a mystical cause – witchcraft or magic – would account for the granary falling down at that particular moment while

WITCHCRAFT, ORACLES
AND MAGIC AMONG THE
AZANDE

BY

E. E. EVANS-PRITCHARD
M.A. (OXON.), Ph.D. (LONDON)
RESEARCH LECTURER IN AFRICAN SOCIOLOGY AT THE
UNIVERSITY OF OXFORD
SOMETIME PROFESSOR OF SOCIOLOGY AT THE
EGYPTIAN UNIVERSITY, CAIRO

WITH A FOREWORD BY
Professor C. G. SELIGMAN F.R.S.

OXFORD
AT THE CLARENDON PRESS

1. A prince's deputy at the court of Rikita. He holds a deputy's knife of office

those particular people were resting in its shade, causing their deaths. Zande talk of the *sa* (tail) and *ndu* (foot) of an explanation, and Evans-Pritchard used the Zande hunting distinction between the first spear and the second spear, both of which are needed to make a kill.

Witchcraft (*mangu*) is the most common mystical cause, or explanation for why, rather than how, misfortunes occur. Witchcraft is an inherited organic substance in the abdomen of some people that is activated by greed, jealousy, spite and other such emotions. Typical consequences of witchcraft are crop failure, unsuccessful hunting, a house fire, a hunting accident, injury that does not heal, illness and death. When misfortune occurs, especially if it is ongoing or repetitive, the victim's family seeks out the witch to have them withdraw, or 'cool', the witchcraft. They do this primarily by consulting oracles.

An oracle is an object or substance that, thanks to its *mbisimo*, or soul, can answer yes/no questions about mystical events, non-mystical crimes such as theft or adultery or success in future events (e.g., 'Is today a good day to go hunting?'). Though oracles are often categorized as a method of divination, in the Zande language there is no connection between diviner (*binza*) and oracle (*ka soroka*, a verb meaning 'to consult an oracle'). Diviners are men who have a sort of second sight; the diviner is the instrument and, as a human, he can make statements about and take action against mystical threats. An oracle operator, in contrast, merely puts binary questions to the oracle. The oracle is the instrument, the oracle operator merely its mouthpiece.

Of the many oracles used by Zande people, we describe just two here, which have been and are still predominant in designating witches responsible for misfortune. *Iwa,* or 'rubbing board oracle', is portable and relatively easy to use. It is a small tripod with a flat surface on top, over which another piece of wood, its lid, is rubbed. When the flat surfaces are dampened, sometimes the lid runs smoothly but sometimes it sticks (*kpa*). This contrast is used to answer questions in binary form. For example, the operator may start by asking whether an illness was caused by a witch living in one hamlet or another, rubbing the lid as different hamlets are named. If the lid sticks when a particular hamlet is named, it means that the witch is from that hamlet. The procedure can then be repeated with a more specific set of questions, such as the names of the people living in that hamlet. A good

opposite

55 The title page of E.E. Evans-Pritchard's *Witchcraft, Oracles and Magic among the Azande* (1937). This book pioneered the study of divination systems in terms of their own internal logics and remains a key reference.

below

56 An *iwa*; board. Questions are asked as the rubber is slid across the moistened base. If it sticks, the question being asked has been answered positively.

operator asks adroit questions based on their knowledge of the social context surrounding misfortune.

The most prestigious oracle, the one used in royal courts, was *benge* (as its use nowadays is hard to ascertain, we use the past tense). *Benge* is both the name of a specific vine (probably *Strychnos icaja*) and the poison oracle derived from the *benge* plant in combination with extracts from other plants. The *benge* plant grows only in south-western Zandeland, so oracle operators had to travel to replenish their stocks; it also became harder to obtain after colonial borders were enforced. The oracle operator would place a few drops of poison into the mouth of a chick after asking a yes/no question about the alleged witch. If the chick died, the answer was yes; if it lived, the answer was no. In the distant past, according to some Zande people, *benge* was administered directly to the accused witch. If the person died, they were guilty; if they survived, they were innocent.

Many factors could influence the result. The poison might be too weak and not kill any birds, or it might be too strong and kill every bird; in either case, the results would be suspect. The dose administered could inadvertently – or advertently – be increased or decreased. The same questions were asked repeatedly of different birds, sometimes in one form ('If it is X, kill the bird') and sometimes in another ('If it is X, spare the bird'). The result was trusted only after a consistent set of answers. Powerful witches could influence the results, so consultations were performed in private, outside the villages and sometimes at night. Self-referential questions were also asked: Evans-Pritchard documented one *benge* consultation in which the question asked was 'Was the oracle lying in the previous answer?'[1]

As mentioned above, a wide range of questions are asked of oracles. These might be about illness but also included questions about where to live, whether to travel, fertility, childbirth and suspicions of adultery. Evans-Pritchard also recorded his own concerns in his monograph, asking who had put 'medicine' in the roof of his house, in other words seeking to identify who was trying to harm him mystically.[2] Oracles are asked to confirm the results of other oracles. For example, *benge* was often asked to confirm *iwa*.

Some fifty years after Evans-Pritchard's fieldwork in Sudan, André Singer, a student of his, filmed what was recognizably the same system still functioning in the northern Democratic Republic of the Congo.[3] In the 1980s and 1990s, I found oracles alive and well among the Zande of eastern Central African Republic. I was told stories of *benge* consultations by elders who had witnessed it. *Iwa* was still practised, though its use was waning, but various household oracles abounded. And Tim Allen, who carried out research in South Sudan in 2005, found that, although Christianity and biomedical explanations of disease are now widespread, witchcraft, oracles and magic 'remain prevalent. At one level, all deaths are still interpreted as a form of homicide, and those accused of witchcraft (or sorcery) are taken to the chief's court.'[4]

57 *Benge* divination. The chick in the foreground has been killed by the *Benge* poison.

AFRICAN
BASKET
DIVINATION

Sónia Silva

In the southern fringes of Central Africa where Zambia, Angola and the Democratic Republic of the Congo share borders, basket diviners are recruited through suffering. Before he becomes a basket diviner, a man (basket diviners are always men) would probably have fallen seriously ill, with symptoms such as chest pain, difficulty breathing and/or episodes of severe mental disturbance. His relatives would have taken him to a senior basket diviner. It would eventually have become clear that all this suffering has been caused by a deceased male relative who had practised as a basket diviner in his lifetime. Such an ancestor, even long after his death, might wish one of his descendants to honour his profession by becoming a basket diviner himself. To communicate with his descendant, the late diviner takes on the form of a merciless spirit known as Kayongo, which the diviner-to-be must learn to deal with.

After such a consultation the senior diviner will inform his clients that their sick relative must undergo a night-long healing ceremony during which Kayongo will possess him. The signs of Kayongo's possession in the ceremony differ from the earlier symptoms, however. This time the young man goes into a possession trance: he makes a hoarse sound, his eyes roll upwards and

58 A basket diviner at work, 1971.

his body jerks violently. At these moments, he is no longer himself. His movements and sounds are the physical signs that Kayongo has taken over his body and personal awareness.

The young man who has almost died from his pain and illness no longer fears the illness now, though he may still worry, for example, that he might fall into the large ritual fire when he is in a trance state or run into the woods in the middle of the night and die there, for Kayongo is merciless. However, having afflicted his descendant with pain and disease, Kayongo now allows him to become a professional basket diviner. That night-long ceremony both heals the patient and initiates him as a diviner.

Diviners develop a lifelong relationship with Kayongo, who ensures that they watch over their oracles and perform the required rites for as long as they live. If they break taboos such as eating food with a slimy texture or engaging in sexual intercourse in the daytime, Kayongo afflicts them with pain and mental confusion.

People consult basket diviners because of afflictions of one sort another. They may have lost a family member unexpectedly or have a relative struggling with infertility or a wasting sickness. By identifying the cause of their problem and prescribing a successful treatment, diviners hope that their divination helps their clients resolve their problems. To do their work, diviners need *lipele*, a term that refers to both the woven basket and its contents – some thirty objects of different shapes and sizes and made of different materials. Some of these are found in the natural world (a rooster's claw, a small duiker's horn, a tree seed), while others are of human manufacture (a metal bracelet, a coin, a wooden carving). Each piece has its own name and symbolism.

A divination session starts with a long formulaic speech known as *kukombela*, in which the diviner invokes Kayongo as well as renowned chiefs, national political leaders and diviners, both dead and alive, while he shakes his *musambo* rattle with his right hand. Following the invocation, the diviner lowers his rattle and readies himself for the longest and most important section of the seance, the divination proper.

Although *lipele* is a common term used in the wider area of the southern fringes of Central Africa to refer to the basket and its symbolic contents, and by extension to the divination that makes use of them, this is also sometimes called *ngombo yakusekula* ('shaken divination'). As this term suggests, during a consultation the basket is held with both hands and the objects in it are tossed briskly upwards. Diviners go through this

59 A basket diviner's *lipele*, 1999.

motion many times during a divination session as they alternate between studying the distribution of pieces that come to rest on top of the pile and stopping to put questions to Kayongo (via the basket) in a yes/no format. For example, they may ask, 'I see a man – is he dead or alive?' They receive the answers to their questions in the form of the configurations of the items after they have been tossed.

To add another level of complexity, these configurations are interpreted partly by their position relative to two parallel lines drawn on opposite sides of the divining basket, one drawn with red clay and the other with white kaolin. In some baskets, the white line is traced in between two red lines. Should the pieces land closer to the side of the basket with the red line, their symbolism takes on a more negative meaning than when they land closer to the auspicious white line. Since most of their clients cannot fully interpret many of the configurations that rapidly emerge, diviners have to translate the material language of the divination pieces into words. Every divination session consists of a quick succession of basket shakings, observations of configurations of the pieces and verbal accounts of those material messages.

During his divinatory journey, the diviner moves back and forth in his search for truthful statements. Suddenly, he will feel a sharp pain in his heart. This pain is a sign that the truth has emerged in his basket and should now be shared with his clients in plain words. The diviner lowers the basket and asks the spirits, 'Do you confirm?' For example, when divining about an illness, he may ask, 'That man who is lying moribund on a mat is still alive – true or false?' Diviners therefore uncover the truth through pain and suffering.

Kayongo is an ambivalent spirit. On the one hand, as mentioned, he forces some of his male descendants to join the divining profession by inflicting them with chest pains, piercing headaches and periods of mental confusion. On the other hand, basket diviners, or at least some of them, see Kayongo as a blessing in disguise. To these men, even though he makes them suffer during divination sessions, Kayongo also gives a highly respected profession and a means to earn a living. More importantly, perhaps, diviners know that their suffering is not in vain. Their suffering allows them to help others who are suffering and need help and empathy.

60 A divination basket containing more than 100 items, c.1850–1900.

SPIDER DIVINATION IN CAMEROON

David Zeitlyn

A large number of different forms of divination are used in Cameroon in West Africa. A widely used form involves tarantula-like spiders (e.g., *Hysterocrates robustus Pocock*, 1899) or land-crabs (e.g., *Sudanonautes Bott*, 1955) in a system called Ŋgàm, which is discussed below. Other forms include casting lots, reading the patterns made by seeds floating on water and observing the way a delicately balanced horn may turn one way or another. These methods are used to answer many different sorts of questions, from who has stolen their motorcycle to who has bewitched their children. How seriously such divining methods are taken varies but one of the most respected methods, which is trusted for the more serious enquiries, is spider divination. Part of the reason for this is that it is seen as being immune from manipulation and, in addition, it is tested on a regular basis; diviners draw a parallel between this method and the calibration of medical devices used in hospitals.

How does it work? The spiders in question live in holes in the ground. It should also be noted that the Mambila people see both spiders and crabs as similar creatures since they live in the same sorts of holes and behave identically in the divinatory process, although only spiders are used by groups to the south of them. In the

61 Tam Umaru, a diviner, cutting divination cards in 1985.

version practised by the Mambila people, a stick and a stone are placed near a spider's hole, which is covered with some marked leaf cards. When the spider emerges from the hole it moves these cards and the resulting pattern is interpreted by the diviners as providing the answer to the question at stake. Questions are posed in a binary form, one option being associated with the stick and the other with the stone. For example, a very common starting point is the question 'My child is ill. Should I take them to the dispensary or to a traditional healer? If the dispensary then *Ngàm*, choose the stick; if a traditional healer then *Ngàm*, choose the stone.'

This may seem to be restrictive, but in practice it isn't. Sometimes both alternatives may be chosen or the cards may be placed between them. There is great flexibility in how such ambiguous results are interpreted. Sometimes it is interpreted as saying that the question should be reframed. On other occasions the pattern of the cards in relation to the stick and stone is seen as giving a qualified result, predominantly one option with elements from the other ('It will come out this way but it will not be easy'). One way of framing the question is to associate one specific option with the stone, while the stick is associated simply with the response 'Divine further'. A single consultation may therefore consist of a sequence of many questions, sometimes asked of different spiders at once.

The leaf cards generally resemble tarot cards. They have a set of symbols inscribed on them, each with a range of meanings. In the Mambila version (*ngam dù* means 'divination of the ground'), these meanings are not referred to as much as in the systems used by other groups. Mambila diviners put more stress on the positions of the cards relative to the stone and stick, as already explained. However, the diviners all emphasize the importance of the cards and their meanings. These can be called on in unusual circumstances. For example, if a card is pushed under the rim of the enclosing pot its meaning may guide the interpretation. In general, being pushed outside the pot is a sign of death.

The meaning of the card may be invoked to discern whose death it is. In this context, for example, the cards for king and queen may be read as senior male and female, and the death as not necessarily being that of a human. In this hypothetical case, if the card with the chicken feather has been pushed out of the pot, it will be read as a warning of bird flu, for epidemic diseases regularly affect the local poultry.

In everyday life, spider divination is used to help find missing objects and livestock, to decide where and when to build new houses and, most important of all, in responding to illness (of oneself or of a family member). Since illness is held by the community to be a result of the malign, supernatural actions of witches, the first question often asked is whether an illness has a supernatural cause. If it has such a cause, the witch must be identified so that they can be made to withdraw their threat. Only then can the symptoms of the illness be successfully treated.

As indicated above, in contemporary Mambila society, this is regarded as the most reliable of the many forms of divination available locally. Other forms are often dismissed as not being serious or as being too open to manipulation. Some people are sceptical of the very idea of divination. *Ngam dù* is used in the choice of traditional

62 A divination result: the stick (and the alternative associated with it) has been selected by the card being placed on top of it.

rulers and is accepted in traditional courts as evidence of guilt or innocence when witchcraft is alleged. Since witchcraft is an offence in the Cameroonian penal code, diviners may appear as witnesses in state courts as well as in village-based traditional courts.

Diviners' clients are mainly local people, although they are sometimes consulted by people who have travelled considerable distances to get second or third opinions on sensitive matters. In recent years they have also been consulted remotely. For example, a client in a big city may call a diviner on a mobile phone, and explain their problems and the diviner can call them back with the results of what the spider has said. Consultation via the Internet started in 2022 (via the website https://nggamdu. org). As mentioned in the Introduction to this book, a Mambila myth explains why spiders no longer talk and hence must be consulted using cards. However, this does not explain where their knowledge originates from. Mambila diviners are very pragmatic and empirical on questions of reliability. Spiders are regularly tested by putting to them questions whose answers are clear, such as 'Am I here alone?' or 'Will I drink beer tonight?' Those who fail the test are rejected and are no longer consulted.

63 *Ŋgam dù* divination cards. The top cards refer to the spider or crab, and the bottom ones to palm trees. Generally, duplicated signs are good and cards with a single sign are bad, but these meanings are not often used.

IFÁ IN YORÙBÁ CULTURE

Rowland Abiọdun

Ifá ló l'òní
Ifá ló lòla
Ifá ló l'òtúnla pèlú è
Ọrúnmìlà ló n'ijọ́ mẹ́rẹ̀rin Òòṣà d'ááyé

(*Ifá* is the master of today.
Ifá is the master of tomorrow.
Ifá is the master of the day after tomorrow.
To *Ifá* belongs all the four days
Established by *Òòṣà* on earth.)[1]

Ifá is the main form of divination used by the Yorùbá
people of Nigeria. It is believed to have been in existence
for many centuries, and is used to address a very wide
variety of problems. At the core of *Ifá* is a large corpus
of verses. In *Ifá* divination, one of these verses is chosen
that provides an answer to the client's question. Verses
from the *Ifá* corpus, such as the one quoted above,
show that *Ifá* is an important repository of Yorùbá
sacred knowledge.

    Ifá functions to restore order where there is confusion,
bring certainty to uncertainty and provide hope to the
destitute. Yorùbá people need to consult often, especially
before embarking on new activities, such as starting a
business or going on a journey. As divining may be costly

for the client – the diviner usually prescribes a sacrifice – only rich people can afford to see a diviner regularly without a pressing reason for doing so.

When consulting for a client the *Ifá* diviner (*babaláwo*) either throws a chain of eight palm nuts or shells or throws from one hand to the other a number of loose palm nuts (*ikin*, a set of sixteen sanctified palm nuts stored in a carved box called an *agere-ifá*). The *babaláwo* does this eight times to generate the elements of a geomantic figure known as an *odù*. The chain is thrown in such a way as to fall into two rows of four palm nuts or shells, each of which can fall face down or face up. Alternatively, each handful of nuts will be either odd or even in number. This is recorded by marks written on a flat wooden tray (*ọpọ̀n*) or on the ground until a pattern with two rows of four marks has been generated. The total number of possible configurations that can be generated in this way is 256.

Once an *odù* has been generated and identified, the *babaláwo* then recites some of the verses associated with it. These are then interpreted to find the response to the client's question. The corpus of verses is large. Each of the 256 figures of the *Ifá* geomantic system has multiple verses attached to it, and it takes many years to learn enough of them to practise as a *babaláwo*.

Ifá was introduced by the god Ọ̀rúnmìlà, the only god confirmed by Yorùbá oral tradition to have been present at the creation and so privy to its secrets. Second only to

64 An *Ifá* divination rite at the palace of the Ọ̀ràngún of Ìlá. The priest holds the *ikin* (the sixteen sacred palm nuts of *Ifá*) in his left hand as he casts *Ifá* to determine the sacrifices that the ruler and the chiefs in the town must make in preparation for the king's festival (Ọdún Ọba). The *ọpọ̀n* is in front of him.

the supreme deity and creator, Ọ̀rúnmìlà has access to
stores of wisdom and knowledge. He knows about not
only human beings but also the other gods, for whom he
has performed divination (many odù verses recount such
divination sessions). Ọ̀rúnmìlà is also thought to draw
on the powers of his fellow gods. He is sometimes called
afèdèfèyò, one who communicates on both universal and
individual levels because he speaks and understands
all languages.

Knowing the principles and laws according to which
the universe operates, Ọ̀rúnmìlà is capable of doing the
apparently impossible, such as changing or postponing
the date of a person's death. Ọ̀rúnmìlà can bring peace
and order to a chaotic world, and is hence called the
regulator of the universe. He can also change the
unfortunate lot of a spirit-troubled child into a better one.

Most babaláwo have an ọpọ̀n, a flat carved divination
tray. These may be circular, semi-circular or rectangular.
They have decoratively carved raised borders, which
leave a recessed central section to be dusted with powder
from the irosun tree (camwood, or Baphia nitida), on
which they record the relevant odù selected during the
consultation. Ọpọ̀n are typically between 27 and 50
centimetres in diameter, and the border carvings consist
of one or more stylized faces identifiable as the òrìṣà Èṣù
(representing the uncertainty in life) sometimes with
additional decoration. These are usually in low relief and
range from simple geometric patterns to more complex
anthropomorphic representations and sometimes even
contemporary motifs such as motorcycles and machines.
Only the face of Èṣù is constant.

Even though most babaláwos own ọpọ̀n, they are
not obligatory. Indeed, all the babaláwos I interviewed
said that there is nothing unusual about making the

divination marks on the ground when an *ọpọ̀n* is not available. This is often done, for example, when the *babaláwo* has travelled and has only the *ikin*, the sixteen palm nuts, which are all that is needed to practise *Ifá*, along with knowledge of the verses.

In use, the *ọpọ̀n* is laid flat on its back so that no shadow is cast on its surface. For both *Ifá* priests and suppliants, this surface is where all shadows of fear and doubt are dispelled in times of anxiety and uncertainty. Through the absence of any distortion and the projection of perfection, the form of the *ọpọ̀n* projects a sense of balance and harmony to *Ifá* devotees. The *ọpọ̀n* is thus a constant reminder that Ọ̀rúnmìlà is part of the primeval order, the regulator of the universe, an attribute that enables him to heal miraculously and to normalize abnormal situations.

65 An *ọpọ̀n Ifá* board, made before 1916. This was used to record the results of casting a divination chain or picking special *Ifá* nuts. The central cavity is filled with sand and one or two lines are drawn in it depending on whether the result is an even or odd number. The resulting pattern is used to select the appropriate *Ifá* verse.

TAROT IN EUROPE

Emily E. Augur

Sometime between 1412 and 1422, the astrologer Marziano da Tortona designed a new game for the duke of Milan, Filippo Maria Visconti, that was played with a special card deck created by adding a set of trumps to the usual four suits.[1] Within a few years, five-suited decks were widely used to play the very popular game Trionfi, or Tarocchi, which is still enjoyed in many European countries today. Soon after its invention, design changes transformed the deck into what forms the basis for today's tarot, which is more often used for divination, meditation, and creative exercises.

Initially, the aristocracy enjoyed playing with expensive hand-painted decks, such as the Cary-Yale (c.1445) and the Visconti-Sforza (c.1450), while the less affluent may have used stencilled or woodcut versions made around the same time or soon after. These printed editions eventually included the conventionalized Marseilles type which had seventy-eight cards with suits of batons (or wands), cups, swords, and coins (or pentacles), and twenty-one trumps and a fool. It appears that by the 1440s, if not earlier, many of the trump images were allegories based on Renaissance, and by association, Roman triumphal processions.

following pages

66–7 Cards from the Pam B edition of the Rider–Waite Tarot created by the Golden Dawn member Arthur E. Waite and the artist Pamela Colman Smith in 1909. In his guidebook, Waite assigned the meanings of 'attraction, love, beauty, trials overcome' to the Lovers, and 'material happiness, fortunate marriage, contentment' to the Sun.

THE SUN.

THE LOVERS.

Exactly when the tarot gaming deck came to be used for divination is uncertain, possibly because it was first used as such by women and for this reason did not make it into the written historical record. The earliest document affirming divinatory applications of tarot, dating to around 1750–60, is a list of abbreviated meanings assigned to thirty-five of the sixty-two cards of the Bolognese Tarocchini (or Little Tarot), a variant tarot deck in which the pips from two to five are left out. Two or three decades later, in 1781, Antoine Court de Gébelin and his colleague the Comte de Mellet (Louis-Raphaël-Lucrèce de Fayolle) published their interpretations of tarot as an esoteric book rooted in ancient Egyptian mysteries. Around the same time, Jean-Baptiste Alliette, better known as Etteilla, wrote of a divinatory technique based on the thirty-two-card piquet deck. His second book highlighted tarot and reorganized the trump order; a revised deck based on his work dates to the later 1780s, after his death a second version was published c.1840, and a third in 1870.

De Gébelin, de Mellet, Etteilla and others inspired members of the Hermetic Order of the Golden Dawn to make extensive use of tarot not only in divination but also in their esoteric rituals. The world's most popular tarot deck, the Rider–Waite Tarot (1909), designed by its members Arthur E. Waite and Pamela Colman Smith, is perhaps the best-known and most influential outcome of the order's activities. It inspired numerous others, including Aleister Crowley and Frieda Harris's Thoth Tarot of the 1940s, and thousands more in the twentieth and twenty-first centuries. The English method of cartomancy (mentioned earlier pp. 128–34), which is practised with a four-suited playing deck, was also an influence on the evolving tradition of tarot divination,

68 The World (*Le monde*) card pictured here is from a nineteenth-century Italian Marseilles-style tarot deck. Bordering the central motif are the four evangelists depicted as animals. This design is also in the Rider–Waite–Smit deck, where it has several meanings associated with success and journeying (or movement).

including both card interpretation and divinatory card layouts, which are called spreads.

The Golden Dawn claimed an esoteric initiatory purpose for tarot but at the same time developed a complex five-stage method of divining with it called 'Opening of the Key'. The consultant begins by choosing a court card as a significator to represent themselves and then, leaving the significator in the deck, they shuffle it while reversing some cards. In each stage, the deck is cut in a unique manner so that there are a few or many piles of cards. The pile that includes the significator is located, turned upright, fanned in the direction that the figure on the significator faces, and the rest of the cards are counted with reference to the numerical value assigned to each. The cards selected in this matter are read according to a list of keywords and meanings, and by other factors such as the preponderance of suits, courts or pips and the harmony

or disharmony of the suits that appear in association with the elements they represent. For example, wands represent fire, cups represent water, swords represent air and pentacles represent earth.

For another spread, called the Celtic cross, a significator is chosen and removed from the deck, which is then shuffled and cut, and the cards are laid to include (1) a covering card (assumed to be covering the significator) and (2) a crossing card at a 90-degree angle to it. Additional cards are laid (3) above, (4) beneath, (5) before and (6) behind to form a cross. Four more cards are laid to one side in a row from bottom to top to represent (7) the consulting person or querent, (8) their house or environment, (9) their hopes or fears and, finally, (10) what will come.

Today, many amateur and professional cartomancers alike find that three cards representing past, present and future will answer most questions. If a situation is particularly complex, they create a unique spread to address it. Furthermore, while tradition decrees that it is better for the seeker or querent to consult an experienced diviner, guidebooks have made reading tarot for oneself very common. The increasing individuality in tarot divination and other practices, including those associated with tarot apps, has further inspired the re-envisioning of deck imagery to align with an ever expanding range of cultural and personal traditions far beyond those of Italian Renaissance allegories and nineteenth-century esotericism, and made both tarot divination and deck design distinctive popular arts.

THAI ASTROLOGY

Jana Igunma

Many different methods of divination are known in Thailand, including numerology, palmistry, spirit mediumship, bone oracle and body mark readings. Among the most widely practised are horoscopic and astrological divination, as set down in two major works known as *Phrommachat* and *Tamra phichai songkhram*. Traditional Thai astrology has its roots in *Jyotisha*, the astrological system formulated in the Vedic scriptures of India, and in ancient Chinese horoscopy and divination known as *bazi*. The Thai term for astrology is *Horasat* (science of the hour).

Phrommachat (from the Sanskrit *Brahmajati*, related to the creator god Brahma) is a Thai term referring to horoscope and divination manuals that were traditionally used to gain insight into the future and fate of individuals. These texts were created to help people cope with the uncertainties and everyday challenges of life. By way of transmission from master to initiate, divination and horoscopy specialists acquired knowledge that was hidden from ordinary people, particularly about the influences of stars, planets, deities, guardian spirits, numbers, plants and animals of the zodiac on the lives of humans.

Traditionally, problems with health and well-being were not regarded as purely physical conditions. In addition

to medical treatments, people would search for the root of the problem elsewhere. A divination specialist would be contacted to find out, for example, if there was an imbalance in a person's well-being or social relationships caused by an unfortunate constellation of planets and stars, or if they had given offence to their own or someone else's personal guardian spirits or certain deities. Divination specialists guide people through periods of change, helping them to interpret unsettling dreams and bad omens and thus putting their minds at rest.

Before making important decisions – such as choosing a partner, naming a child, building a house, moving to a different place, travelling, starting a business, choosing a profession, sitting an exam or setting the date for an important ceremony (e.g., a monastic ordination, a wedding and a funeral) – people would often consult a horoscopy specialist for advice. In practice, certain combinations of the year, month, day and time of birth with the animals of the zodiac; with the five elements of wood, fire, earth, metal and water; and with the male and female guardian spirits of a person could be interpreted as positive or negative influences on someone's future life.

A standard *Phrommachat* manual comes in the format of a folding book, also called a concertina or leporello book. The text is always accompanied by illustrations of the twelve animals of the Thai zodiac, which are similar to the Chinese zodiac except that the Thai version has a *naga* (serpent) instead of a dragon. Four illustrations of the same type of animal, but with different characteristics, represent three lunar months and relate this period of time to predictions associated with these particular animals. The animals' reputed attributes of earth, wood, fire, iron, water – as well as a male or female

69 Two folios with predictions for people born in the year of the rabbit, c.1850, showing: (a) four rabbits with different characteristics, a circular number diagram, a female avatar, a kapok tree as the residence of the person's guardian spirit; (b) six illustrations used for the interpretation of omens related to a person's time of birth.

avatar derived from the Chinese concept of *yin* and *yang*, a plant and a number diagram – are also considered in calculations of a person's future.

Phrommachat manuals often include descriptions of lucky and unlucky combinations of couples, as well as how to use the matchmaking method of the entwined *naga*, a counting method using the image of two or three entwined serpents. Predictions about the future of couples are based on the personality characteristics of the individuals and their horoscopes. Other features that are occasionally included in *Phrommachat* manuals are the rotating *naga* (a number diagram that is used to make predictions relating to building new houses, travel and business) and a Chinese trade ship, from which general predictions are made for the future, taking into account a person's time of birth and certain lucky numbers.

Tamra phichai songkhram is a collective title for astrological divination manuals that foretell calamities, harmful weather, famine, social unrest, assassinations, monetary or material rewards in relation to military operations, defeats and victories. As these topics suggest, these texts were mostly used by court astrologers who worked for the royal family and local rulers. Predictions and omens relating to these events are associated with the appearances of the sun, moon, clouds and the relative positions of the planets. *Tamra phichai songkhram* manuals help the astrologer or divination expert to foresee certain natural phenomena and to interpret their meanings. For instance, sections on military strategy contain advice on what action to take during political conflicts, when there is a threat of war, or when a battle strategy is in planning.

The illustrations in *Tamra phichai songkhram* manuals, which are often of a high quality, are intended as a

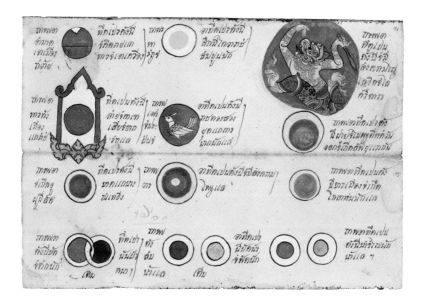

graphic depiction of the textual content. *Tamra phichai songkhram* manuals are usually in a folding book format with a landscape orientation. They were first mentioned in Thai chronicles dating back to the end of the fifteenth century, but their contents were inspired by earlier sources introduced into Thai culture via the Khmer Empire.

Male astrologers called *horachahn* (Thai for 'scholar of the hour') enjoyed a high social standing until the late nineteenth century, especially if they were employed at the royal court and by local rulers, or if they had previously been ordained as Buddhist monks. Traditionally even small communities had male and female diviners, known as *mor du* ('seeing doctor'), who were respected in their communities. In modern Thai society, divination services are often run as commercial businesses.

70 Illustrations of twelve different appearances of the sun including in the shapes of Hanuman, a palace and a peacock, caused by sunspots and solar flares, with related predictions and omens explained in the captions next to the images, *c.*1900.

श्री छत्रपति शिवाजीराजे त्रातोजीराजे भोसले
जन्म: फाल्गुन ता-१९ फेब्रुवारी इखस्ताब्सन १६३० २५ ा७ नाग
स्वस्थरे ज्ञादेगृह कु॥१३५ शके१५५१
साप्तमाली मुर्यास्तानेवर जथ.
बन्या राशौ + हरत नशिक-
कृतरसग + सिहिर ग्र्ुहित:

INDIAN ASTRO-MORPHOLOGY

Emmanuel Grimaud

In India, astrology is called Jyotish (meaning 'light'). The contexts in which such light is necessary to compensate for our lack of vision are so varied that a full life wouldn't be enough to document its techniques and forms, past or present. During multiple consultations, astrologers help their clients develop an astral matrix through which they can think about their lives. Astrologers reveal the movements of this dense, bright matrix and study its whims and intimate rhythms to understand, optimize and expand (bringing the stars into consideration) the possibilities of action. An astral matrix has its own periodicity. Within its frame, positive influences as well as blockages and conflicts due to hostile influences, can be identified. The complexity of decision-making expands radically with the inclusion of the stars, which are recognized here as partners in their own right and with whom an individual must deal. The astral matrix introduces entities that can affect an individual's behaviour. People must coordinate with the stars at certain times to increase the chance of a gain (or from which individuals must protect themselves).

In India, it is possible to draw up the astrological chart of almost any entity on earth – a person, a animal, a temple, a house, a project or even a country, an

71 Diagram and Portrait of Shri Chhatrapati Shivajiraje Shahajiraje Bhosale, known as Shivaji. Date of birth: 19 February 1630 (according to the Hindu calendar, month of Phalgun 31, 1551) after dusk. Zodiac sign: Kanya (Virgo) + 'Hasta' Nakshatra 'Uttarayan' + autumn season. The portrait includes part of his astrological chart.

institution or a nation. Astrologers may be consulted to neutralize the influence of unfavourable planets, for which there are always remedies that the astrologer will prescribe. Or they may be consulted for general help in making decisions, often after previous consultations were found to have been helpful. Some astrologers explore new techniques or resurrect old ones, thus renewing their discipline through contact with new or forgotten tools and media.

One such astrologer was Pandit Kulkarni (b. 1930), who was the son of an astrologer himself. He worked for many years as a draughtsman on archaeological excavations, and was known for his reconstructions of human skulls and his geological drawings. He also drew portraits of people, sometimes without ever having seen them, based on their birth charts, and left behind hundreds of portraits that are the traces of a fluid research process that crosses the boundaries between archaeology, physical anthropology, art and divination. His clientele consisted mainly of women, including sex workers and actors; politicians, mafiosi and gangsters also followed his predictions. His secret wish was to compose an astrological encyclopedia of humankind.

Kulkarni used terms such as *astro-morphology, astro-skeletonics* and *robot portrait* (see p. 179) with reference to his work. He drew parallels between the morphology of rocks, landscapes, human evolution and the ballet of the stars. Above all, he offered people innovative predictive support: his robot portraits show astral influences integrated with the face of his subjects. He considered a person's face, skull and horoscope as photographic negatives of each other, for just as the face is related to the skull, an individual's skeleton (including their skull) itself is related to the movement of the planets.

As well as working with clients in person, Kulkarni also produced conjectural horoscopes for famous people or based on faces reconstructed from cranial remains. This might involve studying the faces of historical figures for whom there were portraits but whose birth chart was unknown. He also reconstructed faces (and possible horoscopes) from archaeological skulls, to which he had access when he worked as a draftsman for the Archaeological Survey of India. He would change his method depending which were the known factor(s) (face, skull or horoscope). This 'automatically' inferred missing details which is why he called them 'robot portraits'.

For Kulkarni each face was a pluriverse, a battlefield where entities, divinities and planets confront each other, a zone of conflicting passions criss-crossed by multiple influences rather than controlled by a single power. Any concretion, whether a face or a landscape, exists in a 'fragile cohesion' between fluctuating forces in tension. As well as giving advice to and creating portraits of his clients, he kept records about them as part of his astrological encyclopedia project mainly in the form of annotated portraits. For example, a man wanted by the police was described as follows:

> Man on the run, date 28-10-1993. The god of death, Venus, is opposite the god of Intelligence and he emerges in Virgo placed in low position. The consequence of this configuration is that his mind has been filled with a desire for emancipation but his enemies have taken over his body.[1]

He described a woman known to stir up the passions of men as follows:

> Date of birth, 19 November 1977 dawn, 6:15 Birth and marriage horoscope: Arrogant beauty. Pretentious woman

with eyes capable of arousing violent male passions. Nature could only have given birth to such a creature in a moment of distraction. The Body is influenced by the Sun and Budh, the Intelligence, influences her face, the suppleness of her structure and her fragile cohesion. Hence also her bright milk complexion of magnetic power, her strong bones and the solid structure of her muscles influenced by Budh. As for her beauty, she owes it to Venus and the influence of Libra.[2]

Creating a portrait both increases and fixes the astral forces by offering a frozen image of the person, thus fixing the grip of those forces. By confronting the subject with the play of astral forces, the portrait makes visible the inescapable current that makes that individual 'a gun', the instrument of an interstellar war that is taking place beyond their consciousness. Kulkarni saw an individual's inclinations and passions as being deeply linked to the cosmos. Paradoxically, the deeper into an individual one goes, the more they must open up to the life of the cosmos.

How does astrology connect resonances between astral forces and individuals to the realm of passions? In Kulkarni's astro-morphology, each trait (*laksana*) includes several possible interpretations that increase the possibilities of 'sounding right' (making positive resonances between personal traits and astral forces). Astrology can be understood as a delicate dance that aims to balance the passions of an individual with the universe, which Kulkarni unusually helped through the medium of portraiture. A person is always a configuration, a relationship between relationships. From an astrological point of view, a body is unique because it is located at the meeting point of forces that may attract, repel or neutralize each other at different times.

The reasons people consulted Kulkarni varied, from possible marriage partners for themselves or their children to treatments for illness and business prospects. When consulting, he used combinations of birth charts, facial examination and palpation of the skull. Clients could then contemplate their deepest tendencies as displayed in their astral portraits. The aim was for a client, once they had seen their astral portrait, to gradually allow it to replace their self-image. Superimposing the skull and face onto the astral portrait completed the astro-morphosis, putting the person back into the field of the astral forces at work and revealing to them the cosmic drama being played out within and through them. Each portrait was destined to appear in an astral encyclopaedia of evolution, alongside rocks, plants and great apes, Kulkarni's drawings published in *L'étrange encyclopédie du docteur K* (2014) are the only remaining evidence of the stellar history of mankind he had in mind.

72 The astral matrix connecting astrological chart, skull and face. Kulkarni's drawings make visible the invisible just like X-rays, showing the play of cosmic forces and enabling people to act knowingly, in harmony with the universe.

CONTEMPORARY ASTROLOGY IN THE WEST

Nicholas Campion

Astrology is a familiar part of popular culture in the modern West. As a practice that relates the positions of celestial bodies to affairs on earth, particularly human affairs, it is best known today through the twelve zodiac signs, also often known as sun signs, star signs or birth signs.

Modern astrologers have differing views of astrology's nature. Some call it a science in the traditional sense because it is a discipline with its own rules. Some call it an art because it relies heavily on the astrologer's interpretation and intuition. Still others call it a symbolic language, a kind of celestial writing to be interpreted, or a psychological tool.

The zodiac signs, which have been a feature of astrology since around the fifth century BCE, achieved renewed prominence in the twentieth century. Each sign is given a complete set of psychological characteristics, almost a personality of its own. People born when the sun is in a particular sign are said to share the personality characteristics of this sign. For example, Aries is energetic and assertive, so people born roughly between 21 March and 21 of April, when the sun is passing through Aries, are energetic and assertive. Someone born when the sun is in Taurus will be stable but stubborn; likewise, those

73 Astrology has long been a part of popular culture in the Western world. In the middle decades of the twentieth century, the *Illustrated London News* featured comedic advertisements for Pimm's that drew on the trope of the magazine horoscope.

born when it is in Gemini are changeable and those born when it is in Cancer emotional and security loving, and so on. Recent research indicates that around seventy per cent of adults in Britain regard their sun signs as a reasonable description of their characters.

This system is well known through the twelve-paragraph horoscope, or sun sign column, a format devised in the early twentieth century for print media, newspapers and women's magazines. As print publications decline, these are increasingly found online. Sun sign readings are predictive in the sense that they talk about the future, whether it be the next day, next week or next month, but they are usually more concerned with current dilemmas and suggesting possible options for action. Millions of readers share the same paragraph, so it is up to each person to decide what they make of it. In this way the reader can be considered the co-creator of the final meaning.

The moon, planets and other celestial bodies can all be added to these interpretive strategies. Many people who follow astrology are aware of their moon signs (the zodiac sign containing the moon at their birth) and their ascendants or rising signs (the sign rising, or ascending, over the eastern horizon at birth), both of which are thought to be especially important. A person born with the sun in Leo, the moon in Pisces and Virgo rising will be a combination of the characteristics of all three signs. For example, they may be outgoing (Leo) in one area of life, shy (Pisces) in another and practical (Virgo) in a third. Ultimately no two people share exactly the same combination of astrological factors at their birth. Even twins, who may be born minutes or an hour apart, share important planetary patterns but not the planets' positions in the astrological houses, representing

74 The astrologer R.H. Naylor, who was famous for his astrology columns in Britain from 1930, also wrote popular almanacs throughout the Second World War. Naylor did not forecast the war, and had concluded in an analysis of Hitler's horoscope that he would not be 'a willing party to war'. In the 1940s the British government worried that astrologers such as Naylor were contributing to public apathy about the war, and carried out an investigation into the public effect of astrology, concluding that astrologers had not damaged morale (R.H. Naylor, *What the Stars Foretell for 1945*, London, 1944).

WHAT 1945 HOLDS
FOR YOU!

WHAT THE STARS FORETELL FOR 1945

BY R·H·NAYLOR

HUTCHINSON

different areas of life, which may have changed significantly. The question of whether twins share a destiny is therefore rather complex.

Today some people consult astrologers regularly, while others do so only when they are at a crossroads, faced with a major decision or a crisis. Clients may ask 'What is going to happen to me?' if they feel at the mercy of circumstances beyond their control, or 'What should I do?' if they want to take control of events. Most astrologers prefer the latter question and try to establish a conversation with the client that is designed to help them make up their own minds – much as a therapist does. Indeed, the consultation sometimes resembles a counselling session in which the astrologer tries to help the client resolve deep-seated problems.

Other techniques have evolved, such as astro-cartography, which projects planetary positions onto the surface of the earth to determine where people should experience certain kinds of events. It is based on the theory that the character of a place changes as time passes and that one can enhance one's life by travelling to different locations at auspicious moments. Annual almanacs also remain big sellers. The astrologer R.H. Naylor published annual predictions through the Second World War, as in the example depicted in Fig. 74.

The use of astrology in politics, once a central purpose, is now very rare, an exception being the US president Ronald Reagan, who took astrological advice throughout his political career. When Reagan selected the early hours of the morning of 1 January 1967 for his inauguration as governor of California, this was noted

75 The US president Ronald Reagan asked the astrologer Joan Quigley whether she could have predicted his attempted assassination in 1981, and she said yes. Quigley continued to work for the Reagan family, providing advice not just on personal affairs but also on matters of state.

in the press and was attributed to his use of astrology. For much of his presidency, Reagan's wife, Nancy, consulted the astrologer Joan Quigley on an almost daily basis and transmitted her advice to the president.[1]

New technology has made astrology much more accessible. Until the advent of computers in the 1980s, it would have taken an astrologer about thirty minutes to work out a birth chart using various tables. These days the calculations can be done instantaneously online, and complete interpretations are also available. Astrologers now provide consultations online, using Zoom and similar platforms, and the best-known astrologers on social media have hundreds of thousands of followers. This has helped make modern Western astrology a global business.

NOTES

Introduction, pp. 8–46

1 Cicero, *De divinatione*, trans. William A. Falconer, Harvard University Press, Cambridge, MA, 1923, book 1, i.

2 Ibid., book 1, iii.

3 Ibid., book 1, xxxix.

4 Ibid., book 1, xiv.

5 Njoya, Sultan de Foumban, *Histoire et coutumes des Bamun: redigée sous la direction du Sultan Njoya*, trans. Pasteur Henri Martin, Centre du Cameroun Série: Populations no. 5, Institut Français de l'Afrique Noire, Yaoundé, 1952, p. 226.

6 Ibid., p. 128.

Extispicy in Ancient Mesopotamia, pp. 47–51

1 Gilbert J. P. McEwan, 'A Seleucid Augural Request', *Zeitschrift für Assyriologie und Vorderasiatische Archäologie*, vol. 70, no. 1, 1980, 58–69.

2 Jean-Robert Kupper, *Archives royales de Mari*, vol. III, *Lettres*, Librarie Orientaliste Paul Geuthner, Paris, 1948, 30, ll. 9–11.

Sortilege in Medieval Europe, pp. 81–6

1 *Sortes* text, *Post solem surgunt stellae*, quoted and translated in William E. Klingshirn, 'Defining the *Sortes Sanctorum*: Gibbon, Du Cange, and Early Christian Lot Divination', *Journal of Early Christian Studies*, vol. 10, no. 1, 2002, p. 95.

Palmistry in Britain and the United States, pp. 105–10

1 Oscar Wilde, 'Lord Arthur Savile's Crime: A Study of Cheiromancy' (1887), in *Lord Arthur Savile's Crime and Other Stories*, Methuen, London, 1909, p. 6.

2 Ibid., p. 16.

3 Vagrancy Act 1824, www.legislation.gov.uk/ukpga/Geo4/5/83/section/4 (accessed 11 March 2024).

Zande Divination, pp. 145–9

1 E.E. Evans-Pritchard, *Witchcraft Oracles and Magic among the Azande*, Oxford University Press, Oxford, 1976 [1937], p. 303.

2 Ibid., p. 403.

3 André Singer (dir.), *Witchcraft among the Zande*, Disappearing World Series, Granada Films, 1975.

4 Tim Allen, 'Witchcraft, Sexuality and HIV/AIDS among the Azande of Sudan', *Journal of Eastern African Studies*, vol. 1, no. 3, 2007, 359–96.

Ifá in Yorùbá Culture, pp. 161–4

1 Wande Abímbólá, *Ifá: An Exposition of Ifá Literary Corpus*, Oxford University Press, Oxford, 1976, p. 10.

Tarot in Europe, pp. 165–70

1 Ross G.R. Caldwell and Marco Ponzi (eds. and trans.), *Tractacus de deificatione sexdecim heroum per Martianum de Sancto Alosio/A Treatise on the Deification of Sixteen Heroes by Marziano Da Sant' Alosio*, with text, translation, introduction, and notes, and illus. from *The Marziano Tarot* recreated by Robert Place, Scholion Press, 2019.

Indian Astro-Morphology, pp. 177–81

1 Emmanuel Grimaud, *L'étrange encyclopédie du docteur K: portraits et horoscopes d'un astrologue indien*, Société d'Ethnologie, Nanterre, 2014, p. 117.

2 Ibid., p. 94.

Contemporary Astrology in the West, pp. 182–7

1 Joan Quigley, *'What Does Joan Say?' My Seven Years as White House Astrologer to Nancy and Ronald Reagan*, Birch Lane Press, Secaucus, NJ, 1991.

FURTHER READING

Abiodun, Rowland O., *Ifá Divination, Knowledge, Power, and Performance*, Indiana University Press, Bloomington, 2016.

Azzolini, Monica, *The Duke and the Stars: Astrology and Politics in Renaissance Milan*, Harvard University Press, Cambridge, MA, 2013.

Campion, Nicholas, *Astrology and Popular Religion in the Modern West: Prophecy, Cosmology and the New Age Movement*, Routledge, London, 2012.

Cicero, *De divinatione*, trans. William A. Falconer, Harvard University Press, Cambridge, MA, 1923.

Curry, Patrick (ed.), *Divination: Perspectives for a New Millennium*, Ashgate, Farnham, 2010.

Evans-Pritchard, E.E., *Witchcraft Oracles and Magic among the Azande*, Oxford University Press, Oxford, 1976. First published 1937.

Grimaud, Emmanuel, *L'étrange encyclopédie du docteur K: portraits et horoscopes d'un astrologue indien*, Société d'ethnologie, Nanterre, 2014.

Guenzi, Caterina, *Words of Destiny: Practicing Astrology in North India*, SUNY Series in Hindu Studies, SUNY Press, Albany, NY, 2021.

Matthews, William, *Cosmic Coherence: A Cognitive Anthropology through Chinese Divination*, Berghahn Books, New York, 2022.

Njoya, Sultan de Foumban, *Histoire et coutumes des Bamun: redigée sous la direction du Sultan Njoya*, trans. Pasteur Henri Martin, Centre du Cameroun Série: Populations no. 5, Institut Français de l'Afrique Noire, Yaoundé, 1952.

Page, Sophie, *Astrology in Medieval Manuscripts*, British Library, London, 2017.

Page, Sophie, *Magic in the Cloister: Pious Motives, Illicit Interests, and Occult Approaches to the Medieval Universe*, University of Pennsylvania Press, Philadelphia, 2013.

Peek, Philip M. (ed.), *African Divination Systems: Ways of Knowing*, Indiana University Press, Bloomington, 1991.

Silva, Sónia, *Angolan Refugees and their Divination Baskets*, University of Pennsylvania Press, Philadelphia, 2011.

Smith, Alexander Kingsbury, *Divination in Exile: Interdisciplinary Approaches to Ritual Prognostication in the Tibetan Bon Tradition*, Brill, Leiden, 2020.

Swancutt, Katherine, *Fortune and the Cursed: The Sliding Scale of Time in Mongolian Divination*, Berghahn Books, Oxford, 2012.

Thomas, Keith, *Religion and the Decline of Magic: Studies in Popular Beliefs in Sixteenth- and Seventeenth-Century England*, Weidenfeld & Nicolson, London, 1971.

Zeitlyn, David, *Mambila Divination: Framing Questions, Constructing Answers*, Routledge, London, 2020.

ABOUT THE CONTRIBUTORS

Rowland Abiọdun is Emeritus Professor of Art, the History of Art, and Black Studies at Amherst College, USA. He has curated major exhibitions on Yoruba art history and written about the relations between Yoruba cosmology (including *Ifá*) and art.

Michelle Aroney is a research fellow at Magdalen College, Oxford, and a historian of science and medicine. She is interested in the history of epidemics and the role of astrology in public health, and is currently writing about the marginalization of astrology in early modern Europe.

Emily E. Auger is a retired art historian and author of numerous books on tarot and cartomancy. She also founded and served as the area chair for tarot at the Popular Culture Association / American Culture Association conference from 2004 to 2020.

Alessia Bellusci is a historian of Hebrew culture, studying the production and transmission of technical knowledge and the history of Jewish magic. She is currently a Marie Skłodowska-Curie Postdoctoral Fellow at École Pratique des Hautes Études.

Margaret Buckner studied anthropology and linguistics at San Diego State University and Université Paris Nanterre. She was a member of Laboratoire d'Ethnologie et de Sociologie Comparative (CNRS Université Paris Nanterre). She worked for the Medical Research Council in Guinea Bissau (1990–93) and taught at Missouri State University (1997–2017). She now volunteers with Partners in Health in Chiapas, Mexico.

Nicholas Campion is an astrologer and a historian of astrology and cultural astronomy. He is the director of the Sophia Centre at the University of Wales Trinity Saint David.

Parsa Daneshmand is a Junior Research Fellow at Wolfson College, Oxford. His research delves into divination, Mesopotamian city councils and the significance of consensus decision-making in ancient societies.

Esther Eidinow is Professor of Ancient History at the University of Bristol. She has worked on approaches to the future in commercial and academic fields and has published widely on ancient Greek divination. She conceived and ran the Virtual Reality Oracle Project, which created a VR experience of consulting the ancient oracle of Zeus at Dodona.

Alessia Frassani is an art historian specializing in pre-Columbian and colonial Latin American art, with regional focuses on Mexico and Colombia. As part of her research on ceremonial language and practices in Indigenous Mexico, she conducted fieldwork in the Mazatec region of Oaxaca, southern Mexico.

Emmanuel Grimaud is an anthropologist at CNRS Université Paris Nanterre. He was trained in astro-morphological drawing by an Indian astrologer and has written about astro-morphological diagnosis techniques.

Jana Igunma is Henry Ginsburg Curator for Thai, Lao and Cambodian Collections at the British Library in London. She has authored numerous research articles on manuscripts, the art of the book and book history, textiles, decorative art and design in mainland South-East Asia.

Napakadol Kittisenee is a historian and anthropologist of Theravāda Buddhism as it is practised in mainland South-East Asia and its diasporas. He is a PhD candidate in history at the University of Wisconsin–Madison, working on the history of magical monks at the borderlands of Cambodia, Thailand and Laos.

William Matthews has been conducting research in and around China since 2012. His PhD and postdoctoral research focused on Chinese *Yijing* divination, on which he has authored a monograph and numerous scholarly articles.

Joan Navarre is Professor of English and Film Studies at the University of Wisconsin–Stout. She co-founded the Oscar Wilde Society of America and is currently completing a documentary on Wilde's 1882 tour of the United States. She has authored numerous articles on the subject of palmistry.

Sophie Page is Professor of Medieval History at UCL and works in the area of European medieval magic and astrology, especially in relation to religion, natural philosophy and cosmology. She is also interested in the visual and material culture of medieval magic and the history of animals.

A. Tunç Şen is a historian specializing in the Ottoman Empire and its many connections with the early modern world. He currently teaches at Columbia University. His published and forthcoming works explore questions related to the history of the sciences and divination, experts and expertise, manuscript culture, the history of emotions and the social history of scholarship.

Sónia Silva is a professor of anthropology at Skidmore College, USA. She has done fieldwork on basket divination in north and north-west Zambia, working with diviners from Zambia and neighbouring Angola.

Alexander K. Smith is a former Deputy Professor of Socio-cultural Anthropology at Friedrich-Alexander-Universität Erlangen-Nürnberg. He is a specialist in the anthropology of Tibet and the Himalayas and spent much of his career studying the reading techniques and perspectives of Tibetan-speaking pebble diviners in north India.

Katherine Swancutt is Reader in Social Anthropology at King's College London. She has been doing research with Buryat Mongolians since 1999 and with the Nuosu of Southwest China since 2007. She has frequently been requested to divine by Buryats.

Pieter W. van der Horst is Emeritus Professor in Biblical and Early Jewish Studies at Utrecht University. He has been a member of the Royal Netherlands Academy of Arts and Sciences since 1994.

David Zeitlyn is Professor of Social Anthropology at the University of Oxford. He has been doing research with the Mambila people of Cameroon and Nigeria since 1985. He is an initiated *ŋgam dù* spider diviner.

PICTURE SOURCES

1   Oxford, Bodleian Library, MS. Rawl. D. 939, section 4, verso.

2   Oxford, Bodleian Library, John Johnson Collection, Supernatural box 2*.

3   History of Science Museum, University of Oxford, inv. 43703.

4   Pitt Rivers Museum, University of Oxford, 1922.67.15.

5   Pitt Rivers Museum, University of Oxford, 1923.20.1.1.

6   Oxford, Bodleian Library, MS. Ashmole 391, fol. 9r.

7   Oxford, Bodleian Library, MS. Marsh 216, fols 26v–27r.

8   Pitt Rivers Museum, University of Oxford, 1930.58.43.2.

9   Oxford, History of Science Museum, Lewis Evans Library.

10   Oxford, Bodleian Library, Sinica 57, pp. 3–4.

11   Oxford, Bodleian Library, MS. Ouseley Add. 175, fol. 10v.

12   Oxford, Bodleian Library, Arch. B b.7, sig. B3r.

13   Oxford, Bodleian Library, MS. Ashmole 220, fol. 86v.

14   Ashmolean Museum, University of Oxford, AN1923.749.

15   British Museum, London, 18,890,426.24.

16   Metropolitan Museum of Art, New York, The Elisha Whittelsey Collection, The Elisha Whittelsey Fund, 59.570.299.

17   Wikimedia Commons/Getty Open Content Program, formerly Getty Museum, Los Angeles.

18   British Library, London, Papyrus 2461 (recto).

19   Rijksmuseum, Amsterdam, RP-P-1896-A-19368-301.

20   Oxford, Bodleian Library, MS. Laud Or. 101, fol. 307r.

21   Oxford, Bodleian Library, MS. Laud Misc. 678, p. 33.

22   Oxford, Bodleian Library, MS. Laud Misc. 678, p. 46.

23   Oxford, Bodleian Library, MS. Arch. Selden. A. 2, pp. 7 and 8.

24   Oxford, Bodleian Library, MS. Bodl. Or. 133, fol. 47r.

25   Oxford, Bodleian Library, MS. Bodl. Or. 133, fol. 7v.

26   Oxford, Bodleian Library, MS. Huntington 212, fols 95r–94v.

27   Oxford, Bodleian Library, MS. Digby 46, inner left board.

28   Oxford, Bodleian Library, MS. Ashmole 304, fol. 36r.

29   Oxford, Bodleian Library, MS. Bodl. 764, fol. 63v.

30   Staatliche Kunstsammlungen Dresden, Mathematisch-Physikalischer Salon. © Staatliche Kunstsammlungen Dresden/Photo: Peter Müller, Inv. B VIII 82.

31   Oxford, Bodleian Library, MS. Rawl. D 252, fols 28v–29r.

32 Bridgeman Images/British Library, London, Cotton MS Tiberius A vii, fol. 44r.

33 Oxford, Bodleian Library, Vet. A4 e.1910, frontispiece.

34 British Library, London, Hebrew Collection, Or. 5557, A66 recto.

35 Oxford, Bodleian Library, MS. Rawl. D. 939, part 5, verso.

36 Oxford, Bodleian Library, Arch. B b.7, sig. G3v.

37 Oxford, Bodleian Library, MS. Ashmole 399, fol. 17r.

38 Oxford, Bodleian Library, MS. Digby 88, fol. 44r.

39 Harvard University, Houghton Library, Cambridge MA, MS ENG 1624.

40 Ashmolean Museum, University of Oxford EA1956.1453.

41 Gottfried Wilhelm Leibniz Bibliothek - Niedersächsische Landesbibliothek, Hannover, LK MOW Bouvet 10.

42 Oxford, Bodleian Library, MS. Chin. c. 9, fol. 2r.

43 IKGF (International Consortium for Research in the Humanities, Erlangen-Nuremberg).

44 Photo © Alexander Smith.

45 Musée Guimet - musée national des Arts asiatiques. Photo © RMN-Grand Palais (MNAAG, Paris)/Thierry Ollivier.

46–8 Photos © Katherine Swancutt.

49 Paris, Bibliothèque Nationale de France, Département Arsenal, 8-S-14395, pl. 52.

50 Photo Tate/© Wyndham Lewis Memorial Trust.

51 Oxford, Bodleian Library, John Johnson Collection, Douce Playing Cards (8b).

52 Courtesy of the National Library of Medicine. Bethesda, MD, HMD Collection, MS B 1051.

53 Illustration © Katherine Swancutt.

54 Bridgeman Images/British Library, London, Or. MS 16482, fol. 1r.

55 Oxford, Bodleian Library, DT155.A93.EVA 1937.

56 Pitt Rivers Museum, University of Oxford,

57 Photo © Stephen Siemens.

58 Arquivo de Documentação Fotográfica/Museus e Monumentos de Portugal, Museu Nacional de Etnologia, R - 13-29-3.

59 Photo © Soniá Silva.

60 Photograph by Franko Khoury. National Museum of African Art, Smithsonian Institution, Museum Purchase, 86-12-17.1.

61–63 Photos © David Zeitlyn.

64 Photograph by John Pemberton III, 1982. EEPA 2013-015-2711, John Pemberton III Collection, Eliot Elisofon Photographic Archives, National Museum of African Art, Smithsonian Institution.

65 Pitt Rivers Museum, University of Oxford, 1916.35.7.

66 Pitt Rivers Museum, University of Oxford, 2004.181.1.80.

67 Pitt Rivers Museum, University of Oxford, 2004.181.1.67.

68 Pitt Rivers Museum, University of Oxford, 1884.100.22.15.

69 British Library, London, Or. MS 13650, fols 4 and 16.

70 Staatsbibliothek zu Berlin, Hs.or. 9565.

71–2 Emmanuel Grimaud, *L'étrange encyclopédie du docteur K: portraits et horoscopes d'un astrologue indien* (Société d'ethnologie, Nanterre, 2014, 2015), pp. 37, 66–7.

73 Oxford, Bodleian Library, N. 2288 b.6, vol. 223, p. 760.

74 Oxford, Bodleian Library, Per. 939 e.145.

75 Joan Quigley, *'What Does Joan Say?' My Seven Years as White House Astrologer to Nancy and Ronald Reagan* (Birch Lane Press, Secaucus, NJ, 1990). St Antony's College, Oxford, E 877.2.Q.

INDEX

Etteilla, 129, 168, *see* Alliette
Evans-Pritchard, E.E., 145
explaining misfortune, 145
explanations and their absences, 26
extispicy, *see* augury

female and male diviners
  Thai, 175
feng shui, 112
forecasting, 16
Forman, Simon (English
  astrologer), 42

ghosts and spirits, 126
Golden Dawn, Hermetic Order of
  the, London, 1888, 132, 168
goralot, *see* Jewish lot oracles
Greek oracle of Zeus, 53
Greek oracles, 25, 53
  lead sheets, 45
Guatemala, 66

Haruspicy, *see* extispicy
Hebrew Bible, 61, 93
  dream interpreters, Joseph and
  Daniel, 94
hemerology, *see* calendrical
  divination
Heron-Allen, Edward, 106
hexagrams, 113, 162
horoscope, 13, 39, 73, 74, 100, 102,
  171, 174, 178, 179, 184

I Ching, *see* Yijing
Ifá, 36, 40, 161
  corpus of verses, 161
  divination tray ọpọ́n, 163, 164
  geomantic figures, *odù*, 162
illness, 24, 100, 102, 149, 152
  questions about, 154, 159

inspired divination, 19, 25

Jewish bibliomancy, 61–4
Jewish dream divination, 93–8
Jewish lot oracles, 62
John of Salisbury
  weather forecasting, 85

Kayongo spirit, 151
Khmer apocalyptic texts, 144
Khmer divination, 141
Kulkarni, Pandit (Indian astrologer
  and artist), 178

leaf cards, 158
lot book, *see Sortes*
lots, *see* sortilege

Mambila, 18, 31, 45, 157, 158, 159, 160
manuals, 62, *see also* astrological
  divination manuals
  calendrical, 143
  dreams, 94
Maragha observatory, 74
medical diagnosis, *see* diagnosis and
  illness
medicine, 16, 24, 99, 112, 123, 149, 173
  Galenic, 100
  questions about, 100–104
Mesoamerican divination, 65–71
Mesopotamia, 36
Mesopotamian divination, 47, 54
  question types, 47
Mexico, 66
Mongolia, 135

Napier, Richard (astrologer), 42, 101
Naylor, R.H. (astrologer), 186
necromancy, 25, 34, 87–92
  against theft, 90

heresy, 91
ritual, 88
ritual, *experimenta*, 35, 89
Nigeria, 161
Njoya, Bamoun Sultan,
  Cameroon, 41
numerology, 77, 171
Nuosu, China, 123–7
Ngàm, 157

oneiromancy, 19, 93
online divination, 18
Ọ̀rúnmìlà creator of *Ifá*, 162
Ottoman astrology, *see* astrology:
  Ottoman

palmistry C19th UK and USA, 105
palmistry, UK Vagrancy Act 1824,
  110
Perennial Questions, 42
Phrommachat, 171
play, 13
playing cards, *see* cartomancy
poison oracle, *see* benge
politics, questions about, 42, 49, 55
pre-Columbian manuscripts,
  ancient, 65, 66
pre-Columbian practices, *see*
  Mesoamerican divination
prediction, 16, 22
  logical conundrums, 23
prognosis, 22, 23, 97
prophet, 62
prophets replaced by text, 62
proxy for clients, 48
Ptolemy, 26
public health, questions about, 102

questions not asked, 45
Quigley, Joan, 187

Published to accompany an exhibition at the
Bodleian Library, Oxford

First published in 2024 by Bodleian Library Publishing
Broad Street, Oxford OX1 3BG
www.bodleianshop.co.uk

ISBN: 978 1 85124 633 5

Text © the contributors, 2024

All images, unless specified, © Bodleian Libraries,
University of Oxford, 2024

This edition © Bodleian Library Publishing, University of Oxford, 2024

Publisher: Samuel Fanous
Managing Editor: Susie Foster
Editor: Janet Phillips
Picture Editor: Leanda Shrimpton
Designed and typeset by Dot Little at the Bodleian Library in 10/13pt Adobe
Minion Pro
Printed in Bosnia and Herzegovina by GPS Group on 150 gsm Gardamatt
art paper

British Library Catalogue in Publishing Data
A CIP record of this publication is available from the British Library